RAZOR EDGE

RAZOR EDGE

The Story of a Youth Club

by

MARY BLANDY

LONDON
VICTOR GOLLANCZ LTD
1967

© Mary Blandy 1967

PRINTED IN GREAT BRITAIN
BY EBENEZER BAYLIS AND SON, LTD.
THE TRINITY PRESS, WORCESTER, AND LONDON

Youth work is peculiarly challenging precisely because it requires a tense day-to-day walking on a razor-edge between sympathy and surrender—*Albemarle Report*

All names of persons and places in this book have been disguised and any resemblance to living persons is entirely coincidental.

CONTENTS

PART ONE

OFF THE STREETS

"Beg your pardon, sir," said Mr Weller, senior, taking off his hat, "I hope you've no fault to find with Sammy, sir?"

"None whatever," said Mr Pickwick.

"Wery glad to hear it, sir," replied the old man; "I took a good deal o' pains with his eddication, sir : let him run in the streets when he was wery young, and shift for his-self. It's the only way to make a boy sharp, sir."

"Rather a dangerous process, I should imagine," said Mr Pickwick, with a smile.

CHARLES DICKENS
The Pickwick Papers

CHAPTER I

OPENING

"Why do you wish to join this Youth Club?" read one of the questions on our membership application form.

In answer to this the kids invariably scrawled, "To get me off the streets."

It was a facile stock reply, the equivalent of the automatic C. of E. which they all put in answer to the question about their religion. The kids knew we would want them to have a religion, so, C. of E. Likewise they knew we wanted to get them off the streets, so, they joined to get off the streets.

Of course youth clubs do exist, basically, to get young people off the streets. They have many other objectives as well, but getting young people off the streets is, even today, their primary purpose.

The streets from off which we wished to get our members were the streets of an ancient market town in the south-east. This old town, which for many centuries had stood in a landscape of lush meadows with a river at hand and low hills in the distance, had over the past hundred years become engulfed by houses, roadways, railways, factories. Southwards it had become linked to another market town which was engulfed by a slum-clearance industrial area which had sprung up round a dockyard. Northwards bricks and asphalt linked our town to a series of once pretty villages which had successively engulfed the next, until finally there stretched, for miles upon miles, an amorphous mass of man-made landscape.

In the early months of 1959 gangs of Teddy Boys, looking for amusement, travelled nightly from the old industrial centre near the dock-yard to outlying suburbs. From each district they were ousted by the police until, by a logical process of forever moving further on, they reached our town.

Elegantly clad in drain-pipe trousers, jackets with rolled velvet-collars, fancy waistcoats, shoe-string ties and wondrous coiffures, they invaded our cinemas and coffee-bars, lounged and swaggered on our street corners. They had no seriously belligerent intentions; they spent far too much money on their clothes to wish to spoil them fighting. But, by their appearance alone, they roused much resentment amongst our local youths and so, in this way, trouble started.

Our local boys contained an inner core of genuine fighters, descendants of Irish costermongers who had at one time emigrated from London to this busy market locality. These fighting boys turned out in fighting costume; leather-jackets, jeans, weighty brass-buckled and studded belts which were removed in a fight and used as offensive weapons, and heavy metal-tipped shoes for "putting in the leather" (kicking one's floored opponent).

These coring-mushes were quite a separate species from the Teds, but in the eyes of the Press and public no distinction was made between fighters and dandies; they were lumped together.

Brawls broke out in our town every evening. Several coffee-bars were smashed up. The cinemas banned teen-agers. Police reinforcements were brought in and soon the Teds, like a swarm of locusts, moved on elsewhere.

Although the Teds had gone, groups of local adolescents still remained much in noisy evidence in our streets at night. Clearly they belonged to no youth clubs or other youth organizations; they came from that class of young people today referred to as the unattached and a few years back as unclubables.

The Youth Service expressed particular concern over these street-corner and coffee-bar frequenters. How could they be got at, as the (rather unfortunate) phrase went? How could they best be reached?

For some time plans had been afoot in our town for an open, mixed youth-club maintained by the local Education Authority; "open" meaning that the club's membership would not be restricted to any particular section or denomination of young people and "mixed" that it would be a club for both sexes.

Perhaps it should be briefly explained here that the Youth Service is run as part of the nation's system of further education. It is staffed by professionals but at the grass-roots level a vast amount of youth-work in this country is done by unpaid volunteers, people drawn from all walks of life who regularly devote much, if not all, their spare time to this activity. Without the co-operation of these people the Youth Service would most certainly collapse.

Education Authority-maintained youth-clubs and centres are staffed by professional full-time and part-time Leaders and professional instructors are engaged by the Youth Service for specialized activities such as P.T., drama, table-tennis, beauty-culture and so on. The Management Committees are drawn from the ranks of the volunteers.

The idea gained ground in our town that the proposed Education Authority-maintained open mixed club might well cater for the unclubables nightly seething on our streets. But where to house such a club? Today considerable sums of money are spent on custom-built premises for youth-clubs and centres, but in pre-Albemarle* 1959 the Youth Service was very much a Cinderella; make-do-and-mend was the order of the day.

So no shiny new premises might be expected for a club for unclubables.

At last, after much search, a disused furniture-depository was found, to let, in a back street. It was decided to house the new club therein.

The street in question was long, straight, narrow; a street of small houses, built for working-class families in the early part of the century. These houses now showed signs of the new affluence; almost every roof boasted a television-mast, cars stood parked opposite front-gates, side-passages accommodated scooters and motor-bikes.

The immediate amenities consisted of a lonesome church, a small general store, a fish-bar and a shop for do-it-yourself plumbers. During the day baths and low-flush suites were displayed in front of this shop; at night they were taken inside and in their place the proprietor stood a not quite life-sized plaster spastic child, much chipped about the face and feet.

Directly the horrified residents of this hitherto comparatively quiet street learned about the proposed youth-club they started a petition against it. This petition got nowhere. Club plans jogged ahead. The premises were patched and prinked up, a full-time professional Leader was advertised for and a Management Committee was appointed.

I was one of the persons appointed to sit on the Management

---

* *The Youth Service in England and Wales: The Albemarle Committee Report.* H.M. S.O. 1960.

Committee. Accordingly, on a windy March evening in 1959 I found myself walking past the chipped spastic, towards the furniture-depository; a grimy and dilapidated building set back from the pavement. It had a large double door in which was set a small single door, in the manner of H.M. prisons and public mortuaries. For a moment I hesitated outside; what was I letting myself in for? But life is a matter of pressing forward, not of hanging back. I pushed open the door within a door and stepped into a fair-sized hall, cold as a vault, with bare walls newly painted primrose, pink and lilac, in the manner of a tarted-up nineteenth-century mental hospital. The place was draughty as the top of Ben Nevis. Several overcoated people stood around, shivering slightly and trying to smile. The Chairman of the Committee stepped forward, shook hands with me and introduced me to those people present whom I did not already know.

The Youth Officer, a charming middle-aged woman, showed us round. "Of course, it isn't what we had hoped for in the way of premises, but it's better than nothing, which was the only alternative."

There was a medium-sized hall, the one I had found myself in upon entering, a shabby, miserable little canteen with no running hot-water and nothing to cook on, a smaller room leading out of the canteen and a large hall leading out of that. All were stark, tomb-cold and newly painted in pastel shades. The lighting was poor. The only heating-system was that of antiquated coke-stoves which crouched, black-faced and awkward, in corners. "They look out of date, but no doubt they'll work perfectly well," said the Youth Officer.

The lavatories were at the side of the premises, to reach them one had to cross a narrow little yard. They were without any form of heating, damp, dank, abysmal; able to pass basic muster with a Sanitary Inspector and that was all.

Their depressing tour of inspection over, the Management Committee huddled into a small committee-room which was embellished by an old invalid-chair and a coronation portrait of the Queen. To heat the room there was one very old, very small oil-stove.

The Queen depicted in the portrait was Elizabeth II but I personally felt that it should have been Queen Victoria. There was an atmosphere about the place which said, loudly and distinctly, that youth work was charity work, youth-clubs places where working-class roughs and scruffs assembled for a spot of improvement by example on middle-class patterns and might the good Lord make every youth-club member truly thankful for what he, or she, received.

The Chairman, a dedicated voluntary youth-worker, was clearly not happy about the premises; he kept explaining that they were the best that could be found, that of course they would look much better when they were properly equipped and full of young people, and in any case it was the *spirit* of a youth-club that made a club a success, or otherwise, not the premises. To this we all agreed enthusiastically. It was the spirit that counted.

Although all the members of our newly-created Management Committee had had some measure of experience of voluntary social work of one type or another (several of them in youth-work) not more than two or three of us had had first-hand experience of so called unclubables.

Indeed we stood, as it were, on the verge of mainly uncharted territory, for at that time there were few clubs for unclubables in existence. The project we had in mind was very much an experiment.

My experience of unclubables was, admittedly, exceptionally stark. For years I had worked in courts, mortuaries, hospitals and prisons and the young people I had encountered had ranged from boys arrested for larky house-breakings to mixed-up kids who burned down hotels, from unhappily pregnant teen-age girls to youths who had done murder. My portrait-gallery of unclubables included ex-Borstal boys Dashwood and Silverosa who had coshed to death an elderly Shoreditch pawnbroker and his dog on a quiet early-closing day, a tragic twenty-year-old boy who had stabbed his fiancée to death in the Old Kent Road and the two young men who mowed down and killed Captain Binney when he tried to intercept them during a smash-and-grab raid in the City (it is after this officer that the Binney Medal is named, an award given annually to a member of the public who displays bravery and resolution in trying to prevent a crime).

I didn't envisage finding youths quite like this in our proposed club for unclubables, but I did believe that a club, open every evening of the week, where young people of the sort who do not normally join youth-clubs might go, could be of value, if only to get the members off the streets, for the streets lead to chance encounters and chance encounters may lead to anything; landing oneself in the family way, busting up a telephone-booth, even to murder.

My experience of actual youth-clubs had been confined to rather gentle, churchified ones in East London. Obviously our new club wouldn't be quite like that, either. But glancing round at my Management Committee companions on that first evening of our meeting together I could not help feeling that several of them probably had some pretty nasty shocks coming to them.

People who engage in voluntary youth-work fall into three main groups. Firstly there are the people who like the young and are enthusiastic about helping them to develop and to broaden their horizons. Secondly come the missionary spirits who wish to save, or at any rate to improve. Finally comes a small group of obstinate people who actively dislike adolescents but feel strangely impelled to *do* something about them. Do *what* they don't quite know, but they are certain that they must *do* something. They are, of course, wildly unsuited to youth-work but they insist upon trying to engage in it.

The missionary approach is highly unsuitable for work amongst unclubables, who resent the barest hint that attempts are being made to improve them, or that they are being even remotely patronized.

We had all three types of people on our new Management Committee.

The functions of such a Management Committee included responsibility for Club policy, finance, insurance, the decoration and upkeep of the premises, the equipment and other Club properties, the selection of Leaders and assistants (in conjunction with the local authority), for liaison between the Club, the local Youth Committee and the local community and also for the continuance of the Club in the absence of a Leader.

It took us some time to find a Leader for the Club. There is a chronic shortage of full-time and part-time Leaders and in this case we had to find someone of special calibre who could work with unclubables. Finally we appointed a young man who had been working at a very tough club in South-East London and

who wished to specialize in unclubable work. He was athletic,
highly energetic, physically very fit; a must for youth-leaders.
He had remarkable qualities of courage and gaiety, a very
fetching personality and good looks, all of which counted in his
favour with young people. He had a genuine affection for and
warm interest in teenagers, especially the maladjusted or
socially deprived; although he nursed no sentimental illusions
about them he believed passionately in the importance of at
least trying to help them to adjust to society.

There are some people who are naturals for youth leadership
and our Leader, Brian A., was one such.

He even had a charming little wife who was a qualified
secretary and whom we appointed our Minutes Secretary.
Brian had a house not too far distant from the Club; he travelled
to and fro by scooter. In fact Brian had everything but good
luck.

The Chairman of our Management Committee was
extremely enthusiastic about the Club and was determined that
it should be a success. In view of the difficulties that lay ahead
he certainly needed all his determination! Our Treasurer too
had an enormous task on his hands for from the first our Club
swung on the proverbial shoe-string.

Local authority grants were made to us to cover what was
considered to be essential equipment. We received something
in the neighbourhood of three hundred pounds; a rather
laughable sum when one thinks of the thousands spent today in
equipping youth-clubs. It should be borne in mind that we
were starting completely from scratch. We had nothing, apart
from the bare premises and a half-size billiard-table and an
upright piano which two well-wishers had given us. Someone
else helped us with a cheap gas-cooker and another friend of
youth gave us a broken standard-lamp which I think the
Leader must have burned shortly after his arrival for it very
rapidly disappeared. God knows what we were supposed to
have done with it! Some folk have a mania for offloading old
junk on youth-clubs.

It was anticipated that our membership would stand, at
least at first, in the neighbourhood of fifty or so. A list was
drawn up of estimated minimum equipment; it had a genteel
church-hall ring about it. Somebody had decided that fifty
young unclubables would require:

50 chairs
2 cupboards
4 trestle-type tables
50 yards of curtains
1 coconut mat for the front door
4 dozen teacups
4 dozen saucers
4 dozen tea plates
6 bread and butter plates
3 large milk jugs
6 sugar bowls
2 dozen tea spoons
2 large kettles
2 saucepans
4 dozen beakers

Brooms, brushes, dustbin, mops, pails, bowls etc.

"Sounds like we're planning a king-sized chimpanzees' tea-party," muttered Mrs Z., a pithy young matron who greatly brightened Management Committee meetings for me with her asides.

A further list of equipment for indoor activities included table-tennis, darts, badminton, basketball, physical education games, boxing. Our unclubables were clearly expected to be energetic. Weight-training we did not think of until later; this in fact was to prove the most popular of all our physical activities.

Equipment for outdoor activities included football gear, cricket bats, stumps, gloves, pads and bag, netball posts and rounders and stoolball.

Of this outdoor equipment I think we actually obtained a football, and the cricket things. During the five years of the Club's existence nobody ever played cricket.

The Youth Officer impressed upon us that, whatever we did or didn't finally get in the way of equipment, we *must* have a record-player and records. This, at all events, was sound advice.

Re-reading this old list one smiles, thinking of the items which, only seven years later, are regarded as standard equipment for even modest clubs; typewriter, telephone, refrigerator, up-to-date sewing-machine, electric hair-dryer, tape-recorder, electric-iron, cine-projector and so on. Such things were quite beyond us. As it was, by the time we had assembled most of the items on our strangely old-fashioned lists, we were running short of money.

Education Authority-maintained clubs are supposed to contribute in part towards their running-costs and the purchase of equipment. The Authority makes grants to the club, usually on a fifty per cent basis and the club is expected to find the rest out of subscriptions, canteen profits and fund-raising projects run by the members themselves. These projects mostly take the form of jumble-sales, bazaars, community appeals and so on. There is something to be said for these projects inasmuch as they encourage the members to work for their club, on the other hand they emphasize the charity-work attitude towards youth-clubs and this attitude is quite out of keeping with the modern approach to youth-work.

After five months of purchasing, planning and talking our Club opened in September. The opening date had been delayed several times; it had taken longer to assemble basic equipment than had been anticipated, the Leader had had an illness. At last however the Club was more or less ready for opening. Even so we had not really analysed the basic problem of how large a percentage of the Club membership should be unclubable and, furthermore, how we proposed to handle the unclubables when they did come roistering in.

As things turned out no unclubables appeared at the Club during its initial weeks of existence. The opening date had received insufficient publicity; that we were at last open was mainly bruited in circles frequented by Management Committee members. Numbers of well-meaning, nice people decided that their own offspring might just as well join the Club; it would be an excellent way for them to learn something, in a well-controlled environment, of the rougher element. By the end of our first fortnight we had a membership of fifty and a waiting-list of ten, but no rough element.

I was obliged to smile wryly to myself when I thought of my visions of bashings and coshings, of vice and violence. The Leader (perhaps also smiling a little wryly to himself) reported to the Management Committee that the Club had had an excellent start with a very high standard of members.

The young people drew up their own Members' Committee and planned a programme of activities. Monday evenings were to be devoted to decorating the canteen. Tuesday evenings were to be devoted to ballroom dancing lessons with jiving after-wards. Wednesday evening there would be "potted sports competitions." On Thursday evenings there would be boxing and rudimentary judo instruction. Friday evenings would be social occasions.

But youth-club programmes have a disconcerting way of falling flat on their faces. This programme was no exception. From out of the blue for no reason at all, roller-skating became the rage. The kids wanted to do nothing but skate round and round the big hall like crazy.

Then weight-training was introduced. The boys took to this with immense enthusiasm.

Efforts were made to persevere with the boxing and the ball-room dancing; a punch-ball was purchased, an expensive buy, but it was hardly used. On Tuesday evenings a few genteel couples could be seen earnestly toiling across the hall floor, solemnly chanting, "Slow quick-quick-slow, slow etc", while the weight-trainers rattled and clanked in the background, but the dancing-sessions grew shorter and shorter in face of the vociferous demands of the roller-skaters.

Nonetheless we were still a club for squares; a few tough-looking boys began to appear, driving up on motor-bikes, but their presence was, as yet, scarcely felt.

The canteen was wall-papered and brightened, the Leader and some of the older boys started to build a Leader's office in a corner of the lounge. The idea was to have both canteen and office ready in time for our grand opening ceremony in October and after several sessions of very hard work this was achieved. By this time the working-parties had got the lounge itself pretty dirty, so this was dinked up too. This so-called lounge was the small room leading out of the canteen; its title was a courtesy one, for there was nothing to lounge upon. It contained nothing but a large wooden table and some hard wooden chairs.

Still, the Club looked clean, and fairly bright, for the grand opening. The actual ceremony was performed by the Chairman of the County Youth Committee, flanked by our Mayor, the Town Clerk, the Mace-Bearer, several Aldermen and Youth Committee people.

As the Mayor stepped into the Club two nice little girls darted forward to post themselves on his either hand and played a surprise bugle fanfare.

Speeches were made and applauded. The Chairman of the County Youth Committee stressed how desperately a club like ours was needed. The Mayor repeated how greatly a club like ours was needed. Several other speakers echoed that a club like ours was a major need. After the last of these official speeches one of our Club members proposed a vote of thanks and there was then an interlude for refreshments. Mrs Z. and I frenetically served tea and coffee; a message came through that the Corporation party all wanted tea please and that the Mace-Bearer took four lumps of sugar in his.

The kids, all in their best clothes, stood round in a state of almost poignant excitement. The distinguished visitors admired the way in which the canteen and lounge had been decorated. A voice, heavy with threat, was suddenly heard, rawly penetrating the politer accents,

"Don't you mess up that sodding wall, mate, or I'll make a mess of you. I papered that wall, an' I want it kep' nice."

It was the first time that any of us had heard anything really unclubable at the Club. Our opening night, in more senses than one.

CHAPTER II

PUTTING IN THE BOOT

ONE SWALLOW DOESN'T make a summer, neither does one young tough make a club of unclubables, but our one, two, three or four toughs found our Club, with its weight-training facilities and its friendly young Leader and its avowed policy of welcoming unclubables, congenial and so they told their mates about it and these mates told their mates.

It had been intended to keep the membership figures down to fifty until Christmas, so that the Leader might have a chance to get properly established with a small straightforward club first and in this way create a firm nucleus for a larger, more difficult club. But this resolution gave way before the queue of eager applicants. By November Club membership stood at eighty-eight; fifty boys and thirty-eight girls, and there was a long waiting-list. Of the eighty-eight young people at the Club some thirty odd were unclubables.

The roller-skating craze had died, as abruptly as it had hit us. But the weight-training was more popular than ever. Magazines on how to develop a fabulous body (male) littered the canteen while male pin-ups, with magnificent muscled shoulders and ballooning biceps, grimaced from the walls.

"D'you really want to look like that?" I asked one enthusiast.

"Look like that? I look like that orready, lady. By the time I finish my trainin' that bloke there's gonna seem a weed compared with yours truly."

He was a skinny young rascal, in a smudgy T-shirt. I looked at him, he looked at me. Then, giving me a great wink as he did so, he slowly raised his right arm and tensed his biceps; what he had.

"There, see that? Fab, innit?"

"Makes me feel all weak," I said.

"Jus' you wait. This time nex' month they'll be twice that size. Year's time I'll be Mr World. Married to Marilyn Monroe an' all."

The girls, meantime, enjoyed beauty-culture sessions.

I asked one of them how it was going. She said, "Well, it started out rather boring; how to have a nice skin, no spots an' that, you know? Eatin' the right things an' not getting constipated an' that, you know? But she's gonna fetch a lotta make-up things along nex' week, an' the week arter that we got a proper hair-dresser comin' to show us all the new styles, so should get quite interestin', you know."

We were still without a qualified assistant Leader, but numbers of well-meaning women, both young and old, volunteered to give a hand with activities. They rolled up in relays; eager-beavers, all dead keen to throw lifelines to young unclubables.

The unclubables had no inclination whatsoever to join in organized activities, apart from weight-training and beauty sessions, and these they participated in but intermittently. Mainly they came to the Club to chat with their mates, enjoy a few coffees or cokes, jive to a background of very loud music and very low lights.

The Leader suggested that the big front room and the canteen should be made available to these young people, purely as a social club; admission to this section of the Club would be payable nightly. Members wishing to take part in organized activities would pay a weekly subscription and have access to the rest of the premises, as well as to the social room and the canteen.

The canteen was regularly staffed by volunteers from various local women's organizations, the female members of the Management Committee and some of our Club members' mothers, but in spite of our vigilance a lot of pilfering went on. At first, like suckers, we canteen ladies put out choc-bars and candies on the canteen-counter for display, but this was simply asking for the stuff to be pinched. One evening I watched, fascinated, as a dexterous youth removed, with a single slick gesture, the entire top-layer of a box of chocolate wafer-biscuits. Deftly the operator slid the wafers into his pocket and then turned casually away. I called after him.

"You may not have noticed it, but you've a lot of wafer-biscuits in your pocket."

"No I ain't."

"Come here and I'll show you."

All the other kids were watching, grinning. For one moment flight clearly presented itself to the miscreant as a possibility;

his glance flickered towards the door. Then he thought better of it, decided to bluff things out and returned to the counter.

"You just show me where I got all them wafers hid," said he, aggressively. At the same time he turned sideways to me, presenting a jeans pocket in which he had obviously placed nothing. It was the other side of him that was bulging. I leaned across the counter and twiddled him round like a revolving post-card display-rack. "Look, in this pocket here."

"Oh no I ain't, it's my . . . " But I started pulling out wafers before he could think of any more to say.

I placed the wafers on the canteen counter in a row. His friends giggled. He blustered.

"You saying I pinched 'em?"

"Not for one moment. Obviously it was quite accidental."

We exchanged a long look. Then he sighed.

"You really want to buy all that lot?" I asked, sweetly.

"No, I only want two." He was regaining his poise. He put down money for two wafers and I handed him two. "Sorry about that," he said, with a charming smile.

"Not at all," I replied, in the same vein. He then left. His pals meantime stood grinning their heads off.

"Don't forget," I said to them, "that everyone of you who pinches something from this canteen is really robbing himself, or herself, and the rest of you lot. You pay for all the chocolate and stuff down here; it is all bought out of your subscriptions. If you help yourselves to canteen supplies for free, then sooner or later the subs will have to go up. Everything in this place is paid for by you, in the long run."

"No's not," said a voice. "Government pays for it."

"Don't be daft. You pay for all these things out of your own pockets."

The grins now gave way to frankly disbelieving looks.

That the Club relied on their subscriptions and the canteen profits for its major source of income was something they simply could not grasp. Efforts to instil in them sound financial facts brought one invariable reaction; not so, the Government pays.

"Don't waste gas, letting the kettle boil its head off like that."

"Don't matter. Government pays the gas."

"Do turn off the lights when you're not using the games-room."

"Why? Government foots the light bill, don't it?"

"You can't make paper darts with that drawing-paper; it costs the earth."

"So what? The Government buys it."

With the onset of the cold weather we discovered how very uncomfortable our Club could be. The roof leaked badly in at least three places, while there was not a nook or corner which could be described as draught-free. The Clerk of Works came to inspect the roof and in due course a builder arrived to do repairs.

Three of the old coke-stoves, upon which we relied for heating, proved defective now that the time had come to use them. Furthermore not one of these stoves had a guard, though the things got red-hot when alight. The Leader let drop heavy hints that the Management Committee might care to consider an entirely new heating system, rather than spend money on restoring ancient stoves and purchasing old-fashioned fire-guards. But the Club was already in the red. Bills for fuel, cleaning, electricity and so on rained down upon us. After purchasing equipment we had only thirty pounds left for running expenses; the coke bill alone cost us twenty-five pounds. So we had five pounds in the kitty for everything else.

Subs and canteen profits were insufficient to tide us over. Finance became our chronic major problem. It was ridiculous, really. We were not a voluntary organization, relying on philanthropical citizens, but a project of the local authority. Yet we had been launched with such meagre financial resources that, after a bare ten weeks of existence, we could scarcely stagger along, we were so broke.

A special meeting was held to discuss the financial crisis. The Chairman asked for fund-raising ideas. Some optimist suggested a Parents' Association. A P.A. would, amongst other things, be able to assist with fund-raising. The Leader accordingly sent out eighty letters to the parents of our members. To cut a long story short, no support for a P.A. could be obtained, either then or at any other time during the five years of the Club's existence. Over this period of five years, apart from a handful of mothers who helped in the canteen, three fathers who served on the Management Committee, and perhaps a dozen or so parents who turned up at A.G.M's and open-nights, we never got so much as a whiff of parental interest (except when we had jumble-sales and mothers appeared looking for bargains). Where, or how, their children spent their leisure hours was no concern of the vast majority of these parents. They simply didn't give a damn.

The majority of our Club members now seemed to be unclubables. Many of the original "nice" members had left; the ballroom-dancers, the fresh-faced little girl buglers who had greeted the Mayor. In their place we had raucous-voiced nymphs in rapier-pointed winkle-pickers, tight brief skirts and deeply V-necked sweaters. Duskily doe-eyed they draped themselves about the canteen, clicking open and shut plastic hand-bags from which they clawed, with nacrous finger-tips, squashed cartons of cigarettes.

On acquaintance, however, they proved to be very much more unworldly than they looked. Indeed they were mostly painfully shy beneath their lacquered veneer. It required much tactful effort to penetrate their reserve, but once they had decided it was safe to be friendly they revealed themselves as touchingly warm-hearted, ingenuous personalities.

One or two of the girls stood out strongly from the rest. Rosebud, a very pretty little sixteen-year-old, was particularly lively. She had a dark bird's nest of hair and huge, all-embracing eyes. She was officially, and most emphatically, engaged to Howard, a pugnacious motor-cyclist of seventeen. They were saving hard to get married and Howard had desperate moments when he spoke of selling his bike. "Marriage means sacrifice," he said. Rosebud pursed her mouth and nodded. "I give up smoking three months back," said she.

Rosebud, for all her childish vivacity, had an immensely practical streak. She enjoyed responsibility and we were able to put her in charge of the subs. She fixed up a species of cashier's desk in the canteen and sat there with the subs book open before her, collecting the money and marking the amounts opposite the respective names with all the hawk-eyed diligence of the proprietress of a French provincial hotel.

"Here, you, you an't paid up."

"I am."

"Come off it. You're two weeks behind."

"Don't be funny."

"Look here, tosh, I don't want no nonsense outa you. Either you pay what you owe the Club, or you get out. And I mean it. S'pose all the kids was to stop payin'? Come on, I know you got it on you." And so on. She always got the money in the end.

Rosebud's closest girl-friend was Cleopatra (not her real name, the Leader and I called her that because of her lean brunette beauty, winged brows and immensely painted eyes). This girl was not only beautiful, she was also highly intelligent, with a strong and witty personality. She was also spectacularly foul-mouthed.

Cleopatra was the daughter of a G.I. who had enjoyed a brief friendship in blitzed London with a pretty W.A.A.F. The G.I. had left for France and had never been heard of again and Cleopatra's mother had died of tuberculosis while Cleopatra was still a baby. So Cleopatra had been brought up, in very poor circumstances, by her grandmother.

She was such an outstanding girl that one could imagine her nursing all manner of ambitions; perhaps to become a model and make a really fabulous marriage, something like that. But in fact she seemed perfectly content with a humdrum job in a chain-store and her only ambition was to marry a straight sort of chap who wouldn't knock her around and who would let her save any money she earned so that in the end she could have a modern bungalow with an American-style kitchen.

Cleopatra enjoyed organizing Club outings; to Bognor, to Brighton, to Whipsnade, to see the London Christmas lights, to Windsor, to Woburn. She spoke of trips next year to Boulogne, or Dieppe, of a Club holiday in Cornwall, maybe even Jersey.

The third outstanding girl was Lana, a charming blonde who had come to us with our first, square intake of members. She was well-spoken, taking O-levels, self-possessed, mature, with delightful manners. She sat on the Members' Committee and played a leading part in all Club activities. At the same time she had a great sense of fun and a natural gift for, albeit harmless, pranks. She had a rare and invaluable talent for being able to mix with her contemporaries indiscriminately; whether they were grammar-school kids working for A-levels, or the beatest of beatniks bumming it between casual labour jobs, Lana could get on with them swimmingly, without lowering her own standards or having these standards ridiculed. All the kids liked Lana and Lana liked all the kids.

These three girls made more impact upon the Club, at that stage, than did any of the boys, although there were three boys to every girl. Of the boys, the most notable was Red, the chairman of the Members' Committee; a highly intelligent, nervously taut boy with a penetratingly bitter sense of humour. He came from a good middle-class home, attended grammar school, but was, for various reasons, under considerable pressure.

Another boy, Clem, bespectacled, dark, quiet, with a pleasant and serious manner, came from a most unsatisfactory home; yet he was reliable, good-natured, generous, obviously (if most unexpectedly) well-adjusted. The one bright feature of his background it transpired, was his mother, whom he obviously loved dearly. He was eternally finding ways in which he could help her.

Fred was Clem's great crony; thin, sallow, shy, with a nervous smile and manner, he was always most immaculately turned out in conventional suits and natty bank-clerkish ties. His home-environment too was unsatisfactory, yet, like Clem, he had a very good personality and showed natural leadership qualities.

Then there was Henry; blond, painfully shy, amiable enough but scarcely able to speak to strangers and always oddly muffled and ruffled in both manner and appearance. He never missed an evening at the Club. He came from a comfortable middle-class home, showed a pathological reluctance to pay his subs, spoke with frightening, abrupt vehemence about his father.

Slowly I got to know the members by the simple, yet effective, expedient of serving regularly in the canteen. At first it was physical torture for me because of the record-player blaring at full-blast all evening only a few feet from me. I am one of those people who suffer real agony from excessive noise; those sessions at the Club stunned me in the early days and I left the place at night feeling as though I had been pounded all over with a heavy blunt instrument. However by degrees I conditioned myself.

A throng of leather-jacketed, blue-jeaned boys and panstick-faced girls bawled orders for cokes and coffees, their voices lost in the din of the so-called music. To add to my confusion there was the difficulty of calculating the change; I simply cannot count and three Mars at sixpence, two fourpenny coffees and one sevenpenny coke out of three bob left me utterly nonplussed.

I needed complete quiet and at least ten minutes to work something like that out. But the kids treated me with understanding.

" 'ere, stone it, didn't you never go to school?"

"Don't tell me you never got your eleven-plus, lady."

"It's painful, watchin' you try to add up. Look, gimme threepence change and take my word for it I'm on the level."

The canteen had two counters. One faced the front hall and was graced by bar-stools, beyond which stood groups of chairs and small tables. Here congregated the unclubable types who eschewed organized activities. The other counter faced the large rear hall; here, during the earlier part of the evenings, solemnly toiled the weight-trainers, or bounded the badminton devotees. After nine p.m. the lights were lowered, amplified sounds from the record-player bludgeoned the air, while couples, never touching yet linked in partnership by, so to speak, rhythmic sympathy, twisted, twirled, shook and jerked like little savages in a twilit, throbbing jungle.

Sometimes boys partnered girls, but often girls danced with girls, boys with boys. The girls, when dancing together, frequently performed with a languor so exaggerated that it was like a parody of slow-motion; this was their so-called cool style of jiving and was intended as the last word in sophistication.

One of the big problems was that of getting boys and girls to mix. They simply didn't seem interested in one another, either within the Club or when they got outside. The boys had their mates and their motor-bikes, the girls had *their* mates and their own secretive, feminine chatter which, every now and again, erupted from secrecy into high-pitched squeaks and sharp yelping cries, only to subside once more.

The unclubables, although spurning organized activities, complained loudly that there was nothing to do at the Club. A Suggestion Box was therefore provided, at the instigation of one of the more naïve members of the Management Committee. The Leader agreed to the Suggestion Box idea wryly; he asked that the naïve committee member should be responsible for opening it and reading the suggestions. The Box died the death after the first opening!

By December we had over a hundred members, at least two thirds of whom were of the unclubable type, and the Club was rapidly approaching a state of chaos. Too late we realized that we had allowed too many unclubables to join at once. The unclubable element, we now saw, should have been absorbed gradually, after we had given ourselves (as indeed the Leader had originally proposed) an initial period in which to become firmly established. Unclubables needed to be stabilized by a good base of clubables. A club composed overwhelmingly of unclubables was not a club at all, in the very nature of things could not be; we were fast becoming what might well be termed an anti-club.

An atmosphere of menace, amorphous, but nonetheless real enough, began to emanate from the members; one felt, when amongst them, that violence might explode at any moment like a mine under one's feet. At first I thought that possibly I was imagining this, since I was inexperienced in club work, but when I mentioned it to Brian A. he said no, he felt it himself.

"To be honest, I'm afraid things are getting a bit out of hand. If I could only get an assistant Leader it would help! Still," he added, "let's try to look at the bright side of things. I suppose this all comes under the heading of experience. And we said we wanted a club for unclubables. Well, we've certainly got one now!"

The members were still perfectly friendly as individuals, but taken in sum they had become disconcerting, to put it mildly. It began to require real nerve to enter that bedlam of leather-jackets. The well-meaning females who had formerly flocked to the Club to help with activities had all left, bar one stalwart matron, particularly determined to fling a lifeline to the damned. She alone persisted; *tableaux vivants*, flower-arrangement, group-harmony, basket-work, she had tried the lot. Now, in desperation, she produced her trump-card; a discussion-group. It lasted precisely two minutes, after which she literally fled from the building, never to return. God knows what she had tried to discuss.

Some of the canteen-helpers started resigning too. Chip-frying was the mania of the moment; one canteen-helper, endeavouring to control a frying session and proving a little too officious, had a half-gallon of frying-oil poured down her skirt. While protesting she slipped on the oil which had spilled on the lino. She fell heavily. This was greeted by howls of laughter. Such incidents did not encourage voluntary helpers.

Brian reached the desperate state where he appealed to the better nature of the Club members. He told them that the Club was like an old woman who had been knocked down by a gang of toughs in the street and was lying on the pavement while they kicked her. If the gang changed their mood and helped the old woman up she might, with time, recover, but if the gang continued putting in the boot the old girl would die.

"That's the situation this Club is in now," concluded the Leader. "So, what are you lot going to do about it? Help, or keep putting in the boot?"

"Keep putting in the boot!" yelled the Club members in unison.

Our Club was in the genuine eye of the hurricane. Nobody knew what was going to happen next. We were disintegrating fast.

A few helping hands outstretched locally would have made a world of difference at this juncture, but they were not forthcoming. On the contrary, we were getting an increasingly bad name in the town with each day that passed. The Club's immediate neighbours complained about noise, especially the noise of motor-bikes. More and more of our members were motor-cyclists. Not the real Ton-Up *élite*; those leather-garbed, skid-lidded aristocrats on their black-and-chromium 650 cc steeds did not come near us; we recruited our members from what might be termed the motor-bike hoi polloi.

These boys were very wild; they were constantly in and out of court on charges of riding stolen motor-bikes, dangerous driving, non-payment of hire-purchase instalments on bikes, non-payment of court fines, and so on. Their unending court appearances were reported in the local paper, of course, and the name of our Club became veritable mud.

To confess, in respectable local circles, to being on the Management Committee was to invite immediate abuse. Everyone wanted to know what on earth we thought we were up to! Our Club, which had been needed so badly, had been such an important venture, and so on and so forth, had become an experiment that a lot of its former supporters were now obviously regretting!

The Leader, in an attempt to enforce discipline, made it a rule that leather-jackets and cycling-gear must be removed on entering the Club front room.

This rule was a popular one with youth-club Leaders five or six years ago; it was believed that undesirable behaviour was donned, as it were, with a leather-jacket and that, upon shedding these jackets, the boys would spontaneously shed much of their bad behaviour. However in the case of our members, at least, anti-social behaviour was obviously more than jacket-deep.

It was about this time that we experienced the first of those tragic ceremonies that are inevitably part of a youth-club's story; the funeral of one of the motor-cyclist members. The boy was killed while taking part in a rally. There was the collection for a wreath, the grim details of the inquest, the sad, oddly resigned reminiscences of his mates as they sat in our canteen drinking coffee on the evening of the day of the inquest, the funeral itself in a bleak, enormous cemetery, the Club members turning up in solemn little groups, far too shy to speak to the dead boy's family, yet sincere in their dumb sympathy.

We now had a hundred boys, twenty-five girls. It was decided to stop the enrolment of boys and to admit only girls, in an attempt to even out the sexes a little. "The influence of the gentle sex may prove beneficial," murmured the Youth Officer, without real conviction.

Of the especially difficult members the worst by far was Rory; a slight, skinny, carrotty-headed, freckle-faced boy of sixteen, who hailed from a well-known local fighting clan. He looked quiet enough when he first joined; he would sit by a stove, pensively watching what went on around him. Then, one evening, he flared into belligerency, produced a dagger-type knife and began flourishing it with gusto. The Leader told him to put it away and not to come to the Club with it again.

So Rory put the knife away. Next evening he brought it out once more. Brian took it from him.

Rory loudly demanded it back.

"Not so long as you remain a member of this Club. Anyway, what on earth d'you need a knife like that for?"

"Cutting my sandwiches."

The Leader put the knife in the box in which he placed all confiscated weapons (there were several). At the close of the evening he looked in the box; its lock had been broken, the knife was no longer within. When the Leader went to get on his scooter to ride home he found that the saddle and saddle-bag had been badly slashed. Rory was not seen at the Club for the next week or so. Then he returned, but without the knife. He seemed perfectly amiable.

Brian decided to cultivate the boy. A jumble-sale was about to be held, organized entirely by Club members. They collected the jumble, put out posters, and so forth. Rory agreed to be in charge of the erection of the stalls; trestle-tables borrowed from various sources. Some of these tables were in poor shape, so Rory promised to fetch a hammer and nails from home and repair them.

The day of the jumble-sale approached; in spite of numerous reminders Rory's hammer and nails did not materialize.

Finally, on the morning of the day of the sale, Rory stalked into the Club carrying an outsize hammer which, with consummate artistry, he accidentally dropped on Brian's toe. He then vanished from the Club for a further period.

The other members exerted themselves rather well over the jumble-sale; they had never run one before and found it fun. They raised twelve pounds, which wasn't at all bad for a first effort.

The Club closed for the Christmas holiday period; on the night before the holiday, December 23rd, we held a Club party. The members, very excited, turned up in force to decorate the big hall and the canteen with paper streamers, holly, baubles and the rest. Everyone wore their best finery. A Group provided music of especially excruciating volume, the drummer and the electric-guitarist thumping and twanging dementedly. I spent the evening washing-up in the canteen. Rory appeared, for the first time since the hammer episode. He looked very spruce. He said, "Them mince-pies and that, we gotta pay for 'em?"

"No. All refreshments on the house tonight."

"Should be, too. Else wheresa sodding Christmas spirit?"

The Group were the last to go. Staggering under the weight of their various instruments they came into the canteen for final cups of tea and the last of the mince-pies. Brian congratulated them on their playing; it had been their first professional engagement. There were four of them and they had only asked for two-pounds ten. We gave them three quid.

Over the mince-pies they now outlined their plans for the capture of fame and fortune.

2

"We get a few more engagements, get people talking about us a bit, like . . . "

"Then we make a recording."

"Costs thirty quid."

"Then after that we get discovered."

"Who's going to discover you?"

"Stone it, we don't know that. I mean, you can't tell in advance who's gonna discover you, can you, till you get discovered? But that's what happens, see; you make a recording and then you get discovered."

Finally, exchanging cries of "Merry Christmas", they left.

"Heaven help anybody who discovers them," said Brian, as we locked up. "My ears are still vibrating from that damn guitar. What's the betting we'll have that old Mrs X. round here, complaining about the noise, before we manage to make a getaway?"

"Thought she'd been round already."

"No, not yet for a wonder. But she will be, oh yes she will."

He was right. Just before we turned out the last of the lights Mrs X. appeared, complaining about the noise on behalf, she said, of the entire street.

Brian apologized and observed, pleasantly, that Christmas comes but once a year.

"That's all very well, but you're open every night of the week all the bleeding year round, aren't you? Once a year nobody'd complain, but I mean to say it's the same thing every night."

"This is the first time we've had a live group."

"Is that what it was? Pity they don't become a dead group then."

She wound up with her customary final thrust that she was getting up a petition to go to the police. After this she left. She did not return our parting salutations of, "Merry Christmas and a Happy New Year."

CHAPTER III

JINXED

THE NEW YEAR started for us with an incident which brought us the worst publicity that we had so far received: Rory knocked down a copper in the course of a street fight. The story not only hit the headlines of the local paper but even received brief mention in the national press.

Our unpopularity in the town sank to an all-time low. Demands were made that the Club should be closed. Persons who, a few months previously, had spoken so warmly of the need to reach the unclubables now declared with vehemence that a boy like Rory wasn't worth reaching. "His sort should be behind bars."

As for Rory himself, he was a new creature. His reputation was enormously enhanced in those circles in which he wished to shine. He had graduated. He swaggered about the Club while the other kids eyed him respectfully. Then he left us, removed to a place of correction. Brian, who took his Leadership responsibilities very seriously, kept in touch with him.

At this crucial point in our fortunes there at last arrived at the Club a woman assistant Leader; Norine B., a sturdy, quietly energetic young matron whose friendly, straightforward manner and unobtrusive gifts of sensible discipline made her both popular and successful with the Club members.

Almost overnight there was a marked improvement in general Club behaviour. This was largely because Brian, who had hitherto been almost physically overwhelmed by the impossible task of running the Club single-handed, was now able to work really effectively for the first time since he had taken up his appointment.

Temporary financial relief for the Club had been obtained by a small loan. As a money-saver the Club was placed on an electric-tariff which cut out our lighting daily between seven a.m. and seven p.m. Brian obligingly agreed to this, although it was an awkward arrangement so far as he was concerned.

The premises, patched and prinked up as they had been for

the Club's opening, now, under the stress of mid-winter, revealed themselves in their true dilapidation. The roof sprang innumerable leaks. Much of the guttering was also defective. Water ran in all directions; pipes burst, tanks dribbled, walls oozed, puddles collected on the floor of the canteen and of the lounge. The Sanitary Inspector turned up. He commented adversely not only on the roof and gutters, but upon the inadequacy of the lavatories and the inefficiency of the drains. A letter was sent by the Management Committee to the local Authority bringing these defects to their attention.

The neighbours were now not only complaining about the noise but also about our smoking chimneys. A sweep was called in; he reported that the chimneys were in such a bad state that he could not touch any but those of the large hall and the canteen. Brian once again suggested that the Management Committee should consider an alternative form of heating.

A letter requesting consideration of an alternative form of heating was sent to the local Authority.

The antiquated stoves, belching soot into the outer air, now began to smoke frenziedly within the premises as well. For several nights the Leaders and members put up with a thick pea-souper atmosphere. On the fourth night of smoke, smuts and confusion Brian closed the Club early and sent the members home.

It was cold January and the idea of opening the Club without any heating at all was out of the question. It was obvious that we had reached another crisis point. A fresh letter was sent to the Authority, requesting urgent help with our heating.

Before any reply had been received, our first Annual General Meeting took place. It was a simple enough affair, held in the big hall. The stove in this hall had so far not misbehaved itself, so it was lit. Management Committee and a handful of other interested persons assembled. However the stove had other tricks up its sleeve besides smoking and during the course of the A.G.M. we all found ourselves on the point of succumbing to fumes. The meeting was called to an abrupt halt and we stumbled groggily into the street for fresh air.

Another, even more urgent plea was made to the Authority for alternative heating.

The Authority replied with two paraffin heaters. These, Brian declared, were wholly inadequate as heating for the entire premises. The rule about the removal of leather-jackets had to be dropped because nobody could in humanity request a lad to take off a warm leather-jacket upon entering our tomb-cold Club. Another letter was sent to the Authority.

Back came a letter referring not to heating, but to the lavatories. The matter of repairs to these was in hand, said the letter. We waited a week or two, nothing happened. So we sent another letter saying, regretfully, that repairs to the lavatories were not in hand. We also mentioned the heating again.

Meantime the members continued to pose their own unclub-able problems. Equipment was damaged, easily transportable items were stolen, a noise-complaining neighbour was baited, senior members rolled in drunk. Some of our young people were in a category requiring definite specialist help; one boy indecently exposed himself at Friday night dances; the Leader quietly turned him out. The boy's parents, when visited next day by Brian, refused to believe that their son had behaved in this way and were un-cooperative. A sixteen-year-old girl took delight in publicly piddling on the floor; on a Club coach-trip to the coast she relieved herself at intervals into a plastic beaker. She too was asked to leave the Club: her parents, however, promised Brian that she would receive medical treatment.

Such were some of the problems that beset us.

However there was now little doubt that the strong personality of Brian and his talent and dedication were at last gaining the day. The members were, almost without exception, becoming devoted to him after their peculiar fashion. They saw how desperately keen he was to make a success of the Club and gradually they began to give him their support. Of course this support went in fits and starts; there were outbreaks of defiance, displays of frustration and aggression, but slowly the tide was turning. Our members were for the Club, not against it.

Brian had a very able assistant in Norine. The kids became almost as fond of her as they were of him. Before long she could do almost anything with them, even the toughest boys.

In particular she scored a remarkable success with an art-class. We had tried an art-class earlier; it had been popular at first, but had then fizzled out. Norine now tried the idea again and this time it caught on wonderfully well, some thirty boys and girls attending it weekly. Girls and boys broke even in number with this activity, although with regard to the Club membership as a whole there were still three boys to every girl.

Of course many adolescents, by the time the evening comes, are pretty tired after a day of school activities, or a day at work in a shop or factory, and it is perfectly understandable, or should be perfectly understandable, that many of them do simply want a social club where they can relax at the end of the day and enjoy themselves. There is nothing wrong in this. Some evenings they may feel more energetic than on others; then they will incline towards a definite activity, but other evenings they won't feel like doing anything in particular. Some of the more maladjusted, or undeveloped ones, will probably never show inclination for an organized activity. In these cases the very fact that the young person regularly attends a youth-club, albeit only to lounge there, may legitimately be regarded as a tribute to that club; getting such members regularly into a club is, in itself, an achievement.

The aim of several well-meaning people at that time on our Management Committee was to thrust all the Club members into activities for the sake of activity, as if they were so many ants. It was sincerely felt that this was what a youth-club should be for. "Get them off the streets and then get them doing something worth-while, instead of idling and lounging."

Pushing is the least satisfactory method of dealing with the young of any sort and it is especially unsatisfactory when one is handling unclubables. Our Leader, who understood this perfectly, endeavoured to explain that Club members should be drawn into activities, rather than thrust.

It was hard-going for Brian; the Club members were anything but easy to handle and the Management Committee contained a distinctly awkward element.

He admitted to me that he felt as if he were ploughing his way into an enormous field of very sticky mud and every time he made progress of a few yards something went wrong with the plough, or he ran into some unexpected hazard. "It's fearfully difficult to make real headway. One keeps sort of bumping into things. Sometimes I almost feel as if there's a jinx around this place. I just can't get going properly. God knows why."

Nevertheless his own manner over the past few weeks and the general atmosphere of the Club intimated that we were at last reaching a point of definite breakthrough. Brian, after five months of struggle, was rapidly acquiring real touch, both with

the Club members and the Management Committee. "Finding
his game" as they say at Wimbledon.

But it can only be surmised what might ultimately have
happened to the Club under this young man's Leadership, for
early in February, before he had even completed six months
with us, he was killed on his scooter.

CHAPTER IV

GETTING TO KNOW THEM

THE BLOW OF the Leader's death was stunning. The Management Committee members and the Club members gathered dumbly in the Club hall on the evening of the day he died and the Chairman officially announced the tragic news which everyone already knew and promised that, whatever happened, the Club would carry on.

The girls were weeping openly, while many of the boys shed furtive tears as they stood around in their cycling-gear. One boy quietly removed his leather-jacket; it was a sort of dumb tribute to the dead man that was infinitely more touching than the loud hysterical weeping of the girls.

For the second time in weeks the kids collected money for a wreath. In a very short while they had got together more than ten pounds.

The sobbing of the girls mounted crescendo. The Chairman said, desperately, "Can't something be done to stop that?"

I went into the Leader's office and found a wooden box full of old pencils and paper-clips jumbled in horrid confusion. I returned, with this box, to the weeping girls.

"Now you lot, you must try to pull yourselves together a bit, you know."

"Poor little kids, they're all suffering from broken hearts," sighed Norine. "They were all in love with him."

The poor blubbering girls stared at me as I advanced with the box. Their faces were reddened, swollen and dumb. Sobs shook them.

"Miss Buss and Miss Beale
Cupid's darts never feel.
How different from us,
Miss Beale and Miss Buss!"

thought I, to myself. I had never felt like Miss Buss before (or Miss Beale either, come to that) but now this ditty from my distant school-days tolled in my ears. I felt priggish, insensitive, a heel. I hated myself. But somehow I had to stop the wretched

40

hysterical sobbing which was rapidly spreading from girl to girl, like an infection.

"Come along. I want you to sort all these pencils and clips out for me."

"What?"

"Sort them out, count them, and put them back in the box in two tidy groups."

"What in bleeding hell for?" demanded the tear-swollen Cleopatra, eye-paint streaked over her cheekbones.

I felt every sympathy for her. However I stuck to my guns.

"So that we can make an inventory. We need an inventory of everything, even pencils."

'·How fucking silly."

Ignoring the rebuke I stood resolutely over the box. Sniffing, eye-dabbing and nose-blowing the girls began despondently sorting the pencils and clips. Every now and again Cleopatra muttered under her breath what a stupid old cow Mrs B. was.

At least the histrionic weeping stopped. But the real, sad tears continued to fall furtively into the old pencil-box.

We closed the Club very early, that night.

There was, in fact, some adverse comment that we had opened at all. But those of us who had made the decision to open felt that the Leader would have wished to see the Club open as usual. He had once remarked that youth-clubs of our sort should be open every night, Saturdays and Sundays included. Were our members to shiver on a street-corner shedding tears for him and collecting for his wreath, while their Club stood locked and dark as a "tribute of respect" to someone who had believed, passionately, in an ever-open door?

The funeral and the inquest came and went. So much money had been collected for a wreath that it was possible to set up a Memorial Fund. A portable stage was ultimately purchased. I am happy to say that it is still very much in use.

One of the stipulated duties of a Management Committee is the continuance of the club during the absence of a Leader. Although our Committee applied without delay for a new full-time Leader it was obvious that for several weeks the Club would have to be run by Norine and our Management Committee.

Faced with this dilemma we all hurled ourselves into the breach. Since we could not contrive to staff the Club every night of the week it was decided, for the time being, to open

2*

only Monday, Wednesday and Friday evenings. An ex-Service man who had had experience of boys' club work was appointed to attend as a second part-time assistant Leader on Mondays and Fridays, our busiest nights. This meant in fact that on Mondays and Fridays we had two assistant Leaders and two members of the Management Committee on duty, while on Wednesday nights there was one assistant Leader (Norine) and two Management Committee members. In this way we just about held things down.

It is not easy for untrained and relatively inexperienced people to step abruptly into active club work, particularly when the club is a tough one. It is, in fact, at first a downright intimidating experience.

The past few months on the Management Committee had to some extent inured to shock even our more naïve do-gooders. However these people clearly found their spells of duty at the Club pretty shattering and they emerged wearing decidedly punch-drunk expressions. Nevertheless they remained impressively game, persisting in coming to the Club and taking everything on the chin. "At all events I do feel I am at least getting to know them," was a gallant comment frequently heard amongst Management Committee members at that time.

During those frenetic weeks all the adults got to know the kids, but not all the adults really liked the kids once they got to know them. High ideals and good intentions towards the young are not enough in youth work. One has to be genuinely fond of the little devils. And just as some people love dogs, and others love cats, and some speak smilingly of the charm of hamsters or passionately extol the sweet disposition of the African python, so are there others, odd as this will seem to the average Briton, who love children and young people.

But even if one does love them this does not mean that one will automatically meet with success amongst them from the word go, anymore than a dog-lover can expect to be recognized as a pal and licked immediately he sets foot in a kennel. There has to be a period of introduction.

I was already quite well-known to the Club members because of my regular evenings serving in the canteen, but when Norine fell ill with influenza and I was asked to take over her art-classes I met, at my first attempt, with total failure. I could not get a single member interested in drawing, that evening. Worse, I could not get them even to talk to me. They drifted out of the room, with those furtive, yet superior smiles that teenagers wear when they are thinking to themselves that you are a silly old berk.

I abandoned the idea of the art-class, went into the canteen and had a coffee. Here I did at last contrive to get into conversation with one little girl. Her brother was going to marry a German and I was given all the details of the forthcoming wedding. Otherwise the evening was a blank, from my point of view. I went home discouraged. The members had been stiff and ill-at-ease with me and I with them.

But on the next occasion I met with success. Several girls were positively eager to do some sketching.

One of these girls was Cleopatra. Another was a lively, rubbery-faced creature called Gogo and the third, plump, bespectacled and rather pimply, was Katina. The others I didn't know by name; I had not seen much of them previously.

No boys were around; they had gone to some floodlit football-match. The girls, because there were no boys present, were much more relaxed than usual. They settled in a comfortable group about me. I distributed pencils and paper.

"What'll we draw?"

"Anything you like," I said. "Absolutely anything you feel like drawing."

This was a mistake. Such freedom of choice utterly defeated them. They stared moodily at their sheets of paper and sucked their pencils.

"I can't think of what to draw," said Gogo at last. "Go on, tell us something to draw."

"Well then, each of you draw a person and we'll guess who it is."

"Ooh, luscious," said Gogo. "I'll draw the Dook."

"Ooh yes, draw the Dook," said all the others. "He's smashing." They turned to me. "D'you go for him too?"

I said I greatly went for the Duke. They all giggled and repeated that he was smashing.

They then watched breathlessly while Gogo endeavoured to draw a portrait, from memory, of the Duke of Edinburgh.

It is worth noting here what an exceptional hold the Duke has upon the imaginations of young people; not only those who know of him through his Awards Scheme, but many others who would never dream of entering for the Awards. There is something about him which appeals very strongly to the younger generation.

The girls sat watching Gogo sweat over the Duke. At length Cleopatra said, "Give the poor bleeder a bit more hair. He's not that thin on top."

"Ooh, he is."

"Blimey, not that bald, mate. Go on, more hair."

Gogo sketched in more hair.

"Now make him smile," said Katina.

Gogo tried to make the Duke smile and met with disaster. "You and your wanting me to make him smile. Now I've ruined him."

She tore the Duke across and flung the paper on the floor.

"Can't we have paints now?" asked one of the other girls.

"Let's have some of the black stuff," said Gogo. "I like that."

"Means charcoal," said Cleopatra.

I went to fetch the charcoal. There had been a sizeable packet of it in the cupboard in the Leader's office. It had vanished. I asked Cleopatra if she knew where it had been put.

"It's in the cupboard, duck," said Cleopatra. "Second shelf down."

"It was, but it's not there now."

Cleopatra joined me and together we searched the cupboard.

"Some anti-social bugger's whipped it," said Cleopatra at last. She tapped the side of her nose impatiently with a filbert-shaped, silver finger-nail. "Christ," she said, with real indignation, "they're a sodding lot. Make you sick."

Some youth-workers are very hot on checking what they deem to be bad or offensive language. I may be wrong, but it seems to me pointless to protest about language that is completely natural to the speaker and has been part of their everyday vocabulary since infancy. I believe that words can only be offensive if used with intent to offend. If somebody comes out with a vituperative string of epithets calculatedly, the one intention being insult, then I will protest without hesitation; but when words, however socially unacceptable to polished society, are used naturally and spontaneously, then I do not presume to object.

Young people are fourteen or fifteen years of age when they join our Club; their vocabularies have long since been formed, certain habits of speech ingrained. It should not be held against a person that they have not had a highly-polished upbringing. A four-letter word that comes out naturally may sound raw, but it cannot logically be held as anything worse. On the other hand, uttered with venom, or flourished like a gaudy pocket handkerchief, it becomes objectionable.

It was useless to object to Cleopatra's language. She was beyond redemption. If one did not like the way she talked then one was best advised not to talk with her.

Although I had been successful, that one evening, in getting the girls to draw and chat with me, I was quite unable to get them to draw again with that degree of enthusiasm. I was upset about this: Norine advised me not to take it to heart too greatly. She said that the drawing-class had had its day, just as the roller-skating craze had had its day; she thought that the art-class had in fact done extremely well to have stayed popular so long. I had come in at the tail-end of it, hence the reason I met with lack of enthusiasm.

Norine now tried introducing basket-work; she got the girls doing this with a will for a few evenings, then they lost interest. She then tried them with lamp-shade making, but the interest was no more than fleeting. Then I tried with rag-dolls. For a night or so the girls made rag-dolls like crazy. But then that stopped, too, and so we were finally left with a collection of half-made limbs, twists of hair, abortive faces.

It is this aspect of youth-club work which so many untrained people find totally frustrating; indeed in the end it often destroys their enthusiasm for youth work and they transfer their energies to helping the old, the blind, chronic invalids; people who appear to be more appreciative and more deserving of the time spent upon them. "I'm disillusioned by these young people; by their lack of co-operation, their total unwillingness to carry anything through," declared one woman who had come to the Club to help. And she left. Her reaction was a very typical one.

The bitter answer is that the gift of getting adolescents, especially adolescents who are fundamentally deficient in education and mental grip, really interested in any specific activity is a very rare gift indeed. And a big element of luck too is required in this type of work; you may hit, purely by chance, on something the kids find instantly (and inexplicably) fascinating and on the other hand you may spend weeks racking your brain trying to think of something that will interest them, only to fail. The great thing is never to get discouraged. If one approach doesn't work, try another. You will find the key in the end. That is, of course, if you genuinely like the young and enjoy their company. There are no keys for those persons whose youth work is solely inspired by a sense of social responsibility, or the urge to collect experiences.

The other major complaint of people who do voluntary youth-work is that their efforts aren't really appreciated; they receive insufficient thanks, if any.

"Modern young people take everything for granted."

Of course they do. They have been brought up to take everything for granted.

Almost everything, that is. They do not take genuine sympathy and affection for granted. These things do not grow on trees for them. But they cannot always find the words to say thank you for them.

As the kids got to know one better they opened up on a variety of topics.

Many of the members complained that they were totally out of touch with their parents. On the other hand equally as many said that they got on all right with their parents, especially with their mothers.

The overall impression gained was that members tended to get on much better with their mothers than with their fathers.

I talked about this with several mothers. They all declared that it was the man of the family, the father, who was the trouble-maker.

"I dunno, we're all alone together, me and the kids, nice and happy and peaceful and then in comes my husband and everything goes haywire. He starts to bully and shout at the boys and they shout back and I tell you, it's enough to drive you mad, it really is. He just don't understand kids."

Again and again women (of all classes) tell you that they can get on perfectly well with their teen-age children because they can still recall what it was like to be young, but the father simply hasn't a clue. "He seems altogether to have forgotten what he felt like when he was young."

Certainly the more anti-social and disturbed our Club members were, the more likely was it that they were on unsatisfactory, if not downright bad terms with their parents, particularly their fathers.

It is interesting that in *The Unattached** the following remarks appear:

Some tension, says this report, between parents and children must be regarded as inevitable as the latter grow up, but "the strains which existed between the unattached and their parents were often far in excess of what might reasonably be thought of as 'normal'. This was particularly true of the relationships with the father: the breakdown in relationships there could be described as acute, while somewhat happier relationships were enjoyed with the mother."

The Unattached asks if, in fact, the breakdown of the father-child relationship is more prevalent than that of the mother-child relationship. Judging by what I have learned during six years of active youth-club work I would say that such indeed seems to be the case.

Materially the contemporary British child is immeasurably better off than his predecessors. Health-wise he is protected to an extent never before known. But the tensions and squalors of his home-life continue often to be intolerable. A television-mast on the roof and a family car at the kerbside does not guarantee that life is fundamentally good.

It is still the common lot of many British children to be knocked about at home, with varying degrees of brutality. Cases of physical cruelty to children are on the increase, not the decrease.

A little brisk, summary execution upon juvenile bottoms cannot be bettered when it is truly merited; but this sort of punishment should be dealt out very rarely, with restraint, and after due deliberation. No child should ever be struck in a fit of violent temper. Thousands of children are.

Conversation with our Club members on this subject were very informative. Many of our young people knew what it was like to be severely knocked about at home. They had also seen their mothers knocked about.

Many of them were perfectly used to seeing father, sometimes mother, come home drunk. One or two had fathers who became savagely drunk.

---

* *The Unattached.* Mary Morse. (Pelican Original). A report of the three-year project carried out by the National Association of Youth Clubs.

I am always much interested by those people who advocate birching and even flogging for young delinquents. Do they really know what a common-place thing heavy beatings are in the lives of so many children? And if these heavy home chastisements have failed, why should an official birching succeed? Do people really believe that modern children, unlike their Victorian counterparts, receive insufficient hidings at home? Fewer people would look upon corporal punishment as a cure for all juvenile delinquency if they knew more about the real facts of British home life.

I think especially of one family whose members were all addicted to violent anti-social behaviour; exactly the sort of juveniles many people would vow could be cured by a good thrashing. The mother of this family was occasionally spoken of by her offspring; they called her an old cow, but they seemed to find her tolerable, nonetheless. Dad, to my knowledge, was only mentioned once. This was when the youngest child, a little girl, at the close of the evening told me that she was desperately anxious to get home. "I don't want us to be back too late," she kept saying. Finally I asked,

"What will happen if you are?"

"Dad'll be waiting to belt us."

"Does he do that?"

"Oh don't he! It's awful," said she, her small face set and pale.

Yes, one was getting to know the Club members. Something about their backgrounds, their reactions, their thoughts.

"You got 'ny kids, Mrs B?" enquired Gogo, as we sat looking at a *House and Garden* together one night.

"Yes. Two."

"Two what?"

"Boys."

"You fond of 'em?"

"Good heavens yes!"

She sighed. "You ever tried false eyelashes?"

"No. Have you?" I was used to the way in which conversation with the girls flickered and darted from subject to subject.

"No. I reckon they'd be hell to peel off once you got 'em stuck on. Give you sore eyes." Pause. "I wish my mother was like you. Mine's so bleeding old. Cigarette?"

"Thanks. I'd love one."

She lit the cigarette she gave me, then lit one for herself. "My parents shouldn't never have had me," she said.

"Why not?"

" 'Cos they're so bloody old. They don't understand a thing 'bout me." She inhaled her cigarette smoke deeply, sighed. "They'd never let on, of course, but I reckon the truth of the matter is I was a technical hitch," she said.

CHAPTER V

TON-UP TAKE-OVER

THE EARLY SPRING weather was wet and icy. Our new Leader did not materialize. The Club premises were bitterly cold, the canteen roof still leaked and the sink drain had been blocked for weeks.

We had a new recruit to the Management Committee, a Mr N., a keen motor-cyclist who had had considerable experience of boys' club work and who now started a weekly motor-bike maintenance evening for us. These evenings at once proved very popular.

Mr N. brought along to the Club one of those rubber sucker things with which one endeavours to unblock drains. He handed it to me. "This will do the trick," he said.

I stood by the sink, pressing this rubber sucker up and down over the plug-hole, while Mr N. talked about the dilapidated state of the premises and how dark and uninviting they looked from outside. "You're dead right," said Cleopatra, who was seated at the canteen counter knitting something small and white, "more like an undertaker's than a bleeding youth-club."

"Young lady, please," said Mr N.

"Any time, duck," said Cleopatra.

Mr N., embarrassed, pretended to start sorting empty coke bottles beneath the counter.

"Real old maid, that one," said Cleopatra, winking at me. "What you doing at that sink, luv?"

"Trying to unblock it."

Lana, Rosebud, Henry and Fred now came into the canteen. Fred ordered coffees all round. Lana said brightly to Mr N.,

"Mr N., where d'you get your smashing aurora borealis sweaters from?"

Mr N. favoured very thick, highly-coloured Fair-Isle patterned sweaters.

"I knit them myself," he said.

"Coo, you don't!"

"What, straight you do?"

50

"Blimey, aren't you clever!"

"I was in the Navy," said Mr N.

Fred said to Cleopatra, "You in the perishin' Navy too?"

"Yeah," said Cleopatra. "How did you guess?"

"See you knitting baby-clothes. It is baby-clothes?"

"If you must know, yes it is."

"What, you fallen at last?" said Fred.

"I'm not the one what's fallen, she is," said Cleopatra, gesturing with the knitting at Rosebud.

"Sorright for her," said Fred. "She's married. She can fall as much as she wants, now."

Rosebud and Howard had married some six weeks previously. They still came to the Club quite regularly, nevertheless. They were at present living with Rosebud's mother.

"You didn't waste no time getting on with the job, did you Rosy?" said Henry. Rosebud giggled and looked very happy.

"We're all knitting her baby-clothes," said Cleopatra. "Gogo, Kat, me; all knitting her things. She'll get such a bloody great layette she'll be able to fit out quins."

Mr N. looked up from the empties, ready to protest again, but at that moment shouts and banging came from the front-entrance and he decided that this matter was of greater importance than Cleopatra's vocabulary. He hurried away shouting, "Hey, there, you chaps, what's up?"

The conversation about baby-clothes now became outrageous. I devoted myself to the sink, pretending not to hear. They were hoping for a reaction from me and therefore a reaction was the last thing to give them.

The wise-cracking then turned to playful barging and shoving and a game of scuffling football was started with Cleopatra's ball of knitting-wool. She shrieked shrilly.

"Stop it, I don't want to have to wash all the clothes before the poor little nipper's even been born," said Rosebud.

Giggling and scuffling they made their way, like gambolling puppies, into the hall. I swabbed down the canteen-counter and washed some cups. The blocked sink made hygienic methods rather difficult. I began working away with the sucker again. Katina came lounging in. She had on a new white sweater and her hair was built up intricately and lacquered stiff. She was obviously dressed to kill. I wondered about the identity of her intended victim.

"Hello Mrs B."

I said hello.

"What in hell you doing?"

"Trying to unblock this sink."

Katina lit a cigarette, sighed wearily and sat watching me for a while. Then: "Like a cup of coffee with me?"

"Love it," I said.

I abandoned the sink, made two coffees and leant against the counter my side while Katina, perched on a stool her side, offered me a cigarette. Several of the girls liked to treat one to cigarettes, coffees. It helped them to feel on a footing of friendly equality.

Katina began to talk. She was having boy-friend trouble. "I don't know what to do. My eyes are that green. You see, he's taking out another girl. Not that I think he's serious about her. Just gone off me. You know?"

I sympathized.

Someone came into the canteen, said it was nine o'clock and might they now put the record-player on? Without more ado they put it on. Sound blasted us. Dim figures appeared in the rear-hall, jiving. Katina, her voice raised to a shriek, continued imparting intimacies about her boy-friend. "I'm not letting him see how it's getting me down. I'm playing it very cool. Least, trying to. Let him think I don't care. You know?"

"That's right. Try a bit of psychological treatment!" I bellowed back.

Mr N. returned. He shouted a request for coffee. Then he went to the back of the canteen and wearily propped himself against a brush-and-broom cupboard. What was it someone said about youth-club work? That unless it's half killing you then you're not doing it properly?

I busied myself making more coffee.

"It's really got me down. I feel real cheesed with everything!" screeched Katina. "Even me hair's got the hump. You know, can't do nothing with it."

"Nothing like being in love to make you miserable!" I yelled.

"You ever get like that over a chap?"

"Make my coffee strong and black!" roared Mr N. from the shelter of the brush-and-broom cupboard.

I handed him a black coffee; it was Instant and had that

peculiar, nondescript flavour that all youth-club coffee seems to have, however carefully it is made.

"You say you're psychic?" shouted Mr N. as he took the coffee from me.

"No. Why?"

"I thought I heard you telling that girl there something about you were psychic."

"No. I said psychology."

He gestured for the sugar. I fetched it for him.

"Are *you* psychic?" I shouted at him.

"Indeed yes. Very!"

The music thumped, thudded, jolted. Katina had taken a round shaving-mirror from her handbag (it is amazing what girls get into their handbags) and was examining her spots minutely in the magnifying side of it.

Mr N. began confiding, at full-pitch of his voice, his lips close to my ear, "I foretold my mother's death to the exact hour four years before it happened."

"Good heavens!"

"Make me another coffee, duck!" sang out Katina, powdering over her spots.

I shuttled madly between Katina, the gas-cooker and Mr N., trying to pay simultaneous attention to all three.

"It was terrible to know what was going to happen: I foresaw the whole thing in detail, you know, even the pattern on the bed-spread . . . "

"If he comes in now along of his mates I shall take no notice of him."

"When I told my sister that mother was going to die she refused to believe it, in fact she was downright . . . "

"When you was in love, Mrs B., did you . . . "

"Imagine my horror, though of course I knew in my heart of hearts it was inevitable . . . "

"It's made my face so much worse too, all this worry about him. I haven't eaten nothing for days, so it can't be my stomach's out of order."

"I got a telegram, saying she had suddenly been seized with a . . . "

"Wheresa sugar, Mrs B.?"

I gave Katina the sugar. "Too much won't help your complexion," I warned her. She slowly trickled a large spoonful into her coffee. "Funny thing is, I don't even know whether I really want that gink back or not."

She huddled moodily over her coffee, clinking her spoon against the side of her cup. I returned to Mr N. who was looking neglected. "I'm so sorry; you were saying that you got a telegram . . . "

"Yes, a telegram. Saying precisely what I had been dreading for the past four years. They rushed her into hospital, but she returned home to die. It was exactly all as I had foreseen."

The music thumped, Katina sighed over her coffee. Mr N. and I stood, oblivious, by the brush-and-broom cupboard while he detailed his mother's death-bed scene. Tears shone in his eyes; I felt them pricking mine. I am a great one for weeping in sympathy.

Then I heard Katina calling, "Mrs B., Mrs B., the old bag's here; I think she's wanting you!" Looking up I saw our neighbour, Mrs X., striding determinedly towards me. She carried a newspaper-wrapped parcel, some eighteen inches in length.

"Mrs B., I want you to take a look at what I just found in my dustbin," said Mrs X.

"Oh no," I breathed to myself, "oh *no!*"

I had, in my mortuary days, seen many such newspaper-wrapped parcels, of precisely that size and shape, and I knew only too well what such parcels invariably contained. As Mrs X., trembling with indignation, placed the parcel on the canteen counter and started to undo it I knew I was about to set eyes on a dead baby; either still-born or an infanticide.

Katina and Mr N. craned forward, horribly fascinated, as Mrs X. unwound the wrappings.

"Just see how you'd like to find this in your dustbin," she kept saying.

"Leave us, would you Kat dear, for a moment?" I said, trying to sound icily calm.

"No, let her see. They may be hers," snapped Mrs X.

They? Twins!

More newspaper curled to the floor. The music throbbed on in the background. Katina began to giggle and glanced at me. It was like a hideous party-game of musical-parcels.

"There, d'you ever see anything so nasty as that?" demanded Mrs X., with, it must be confessed, immense relish.

As she spoke she drew from the parcel a pair of heavily soiled panties.

Enormous relief was my immediate sensation. I drew a deep breath as one automatically does after a narrow shave of any kind. Katina was sniggering uncontrollably. Poor Mr N. stared at the panties as if hypnotized. Mrs X. watched my face closely. She accepted my silence as one of stunned horror.

"I knew you'd feel like that," she said, deeply satisfied. "Far from nice to find in your dustbin, eh?"

"Very nasty," I said, at last.

"I thought I'd show you. I said to myself shall I let it pass and say nothing and then I thought to myself no show them to one of the Management Committee; let 'em see what goes on at their precious youth-club."

"Quite right . . . Look here Katina, either pull yourself together and shut up giggling, or scram."

Katina rolled her eyes wildly at me and screwed her face up tightly in an effort to stop laughing. I continued, "At the same time, with all due respect Mrs X., there's nothing whatever to indicate that these panties do in fact belong to anyone from our Club."

"Good heavens, Mrs B., your boys was all out there in the street playing football with 'em earlier on, with the girl screaming her head off to get 'em back. I was watching through the front window."

"Did you recognize the girl?"

"No, I couldn't make her out that well, but I could see her stood there, and hear her screaming. Then I went to the back of the house to get my old man's supper and I heard feet running up my back-passage and then I heard the dustbin lid go so I thought to myself, 'More mischief! I'll give it a minute,' I thought, so I did, and then I went to look. I picked up the dustbin lid that was lying half put back on, and found this parcel."

Mr N. and I apologized profusely on behalf of the Club. Mr. N. then escorted Mrs X. to her front-door. I spoke a few crisp words to Katina, who was deep in giggles again. The girl gasped, "But Mrs B., did you hear her say she heard feet running up her back-passage?"

Naturally we never discovered who was the original owner of the panties. Indeed we made as little of the incident as possible. The flatter a prank like that falls, the better.

Such was a specimen evening at the Club.

No two evenings were ever alike, of course; variety is a basic ingredient of youth-club work. But one could be quite sure that no spell of duty spent at the Club would be dull.

It was at this point that we became, literally overnight, invaded by the Ton-Up boys. For some time our motor-bike maintenance sessions had been enjoying increasing popularity with the biking kids in general; now we found that we were dramatically In with the Ton-Up *élite*.

Leather-garbed, skid-lidded, zip-booted, gauntlet-gloved, they lined up their big, gleaming 650 cc's outside the Club and strolled languidly into our canteen, calling greetings to their mates. They were in the seventeen to twenty-one age-group; mostly about nineteen or twenty.

Although they couldn't care less about drawing-class, boys' supper-club, table-tennis and so on, they were not averse to darts or snooker and one or two of them became interested in weight-training. They were definitely, though surprisingly, very interested in the organization of the Club as a club. They were boys of decidedly different calibre from our other cycling members; considerably more intelligent, mature and poised in manner, self-disciplined, with qualities of leadership which should have delighted any Youth Officer on the look-out for potential youth-leaders. Before we knew where we were they had virtually taken over the Club and were more or less running it themselves, with smooth efficiency.

The dream-club of every leader is, of course, the club which is to all intents and purposes organized and democratically run by the club members themselves. Such a club is exceedingly rare; although most young people are capable of running some activities themselves, of conducting the affairs of a Members' Committee, of planning outings, even club-holidays, and so on, they invariably fail when it comes to sustained effort. They can succeed with various enterprises over relatively short periods of time but their enthusiasm, quick to be roused, proves equally quick to subside. Thus the youth-club that is run by the members themselves with the minimum of adult guidance over a lengthy period is something quite unique. Now we had such a club.

The Ton-Ups reorganized and revitalized the flagging Members' Committee, organized week-end rallies and outings, ran house-to-house collections for Oxfam and spastics, unblocked the canteen sink, redecorated the canteen, held several financially profitable Friday night dances.

It is true that the Club became increasingly over-crowded and appallingly noisy, but fights, canteen-pilfering and non-payment of subs declined almost to vanishing point.

One reason for improvement in general Club behaviour was that the Ton-Ups didn't drink. Whereas we had previously been bothered not a little by a group of regularly slightly drunk senior members we now enjoyed the influence of the coffee-swilling 650 cc bombers who had to stay sober if they wished to stay alive.

The Ton-Ups prided themselves upon their self-control, quick reflexes and skilful riding. They maintained that they entertained higher standards than other road users. Skilled Ton-Ups who were involved in accidents were rarely, if ever, to blame, they alleged. Although a high percentage of motor-cyclists were injured and killed these things happened before they had had a chance to graduate, as it were, into the *élite*.

They admitted that there were some Ton-Up groups to which you couldn't belong unless you had been involved in a certain number of smashes, but the top Ton-Ups prided themselves on not becoming involved in smashes and therefore upon being superior to such gimmicky groups.

The celebrated Ton-Up games such as Last-Through-The-Traffic-Lights and Chicken Runs were not played by our lot. They scorned such juvenescence.

Still, said our Ton-Ups, the roads being what they are today, you could scarcely hope to get away trouble-free for ever. And indeed from time to time a Ton-Up would appear in our canteen dramatically bandaged. Every now and again some boy or other would go round the Club shaking an old Oxo tin which was temporarily being used as a collecting box. "Come on, Mrs B., you know Clive (Bill-Bob-Tony-Arthur) don't you?"

"Yes. Why, what's happened to him?"

"He's had a smash-up. Curly an' me's going to visit him in hospital tomorrow and we wanta take him something nice from us all."

And on at least one occasion they collected for a wreath.

I noticed that the serious and fatal accidents were forgotten very quickly. Doubtless they had to be; in a way it was like war-time.

They were serious about pure speed to the point of being high-minded. They worshipped speed for the sense of freedom it gave them. A burn-up liberated them from the frustrations of the tediously over-organized, inhibiting and hypocritical adult world which they rejected.

Some Ton-Ups, of course, were not able to say much about their riding, or perhaps preferred not to say much, merely remarking, "It gives me a great feeling to get out there and bomb", or, "Whenever I do a ton I get a kinda special feeling." One boy claimed that it soothed him: "Faster I go the more relaxed I feel." Others, however, once their confidence was won and they felt that you were really friendly and interested, would hold forth in an almost romantic vein. One hefty, leather-clad youth, blunt-featured and blue-eyed, who did not look particularly sensitive, let alone poetic, got really carried away by eloquence one evening.

"I like that feeling all England belongs to me. All the roads are open to me if I want them. You know? I've explored every inch of road in Kent, Sussex. An' Surrey I know like the back of my hand: all those quiet little leafy lanes; I done 'em all. Last summer me and two mates went West; Devon an' Cornwall. Well, it was getting more into autumn, like. We rode all round the coast. We used to get up early in the morning and swim in the sea, in them little bays, with nothing on. It was perishing cold but I'm telling you it was bloody fabulous. It's fabulous, swimming with nothing on. You ever done it? You couldn't think a pair of swimming-trunks'd make that difference but they do. All them waves, they feel quite different when you got nothing on. It was all misty like, too; so early, you see. Sky an' sea all misty. It sounds crazy now, but it was really great. We're going to Cornwall again this year; get right to Land's End this time. I mean to go right up North some time too. I never bin yet. That must really be something; the Highlands."

The Club membership became increasingly male, because as one boy put it, "You can't run a bike *and* a bird." There was never any doubt about the choice; it became a frequent sight to see some girl sitting in a corner, crying, with a group of her mates trying to comfort her. "What's the matter with poor Nina?" "Her boy-friend's bought a new bike and he says he can't afford her no more."

Poor little birds; they could not compete with the glamour of

650 cc motor-bikes in gleaming black-and-chromium; the dream vehicle of every right-minded Ton-Up.

The Ton-Ups in fact were downright austere in their devotion to speed. Drinking was out, birds were out. Cigarettes had to be rationed because you couldn't afford heavy H.P. instalments on a bike and the rest of the gear *and* indulge in heavy smoking.

The better a bloke's bike and gear the better his status amongst his mates. But the final acid test was how well he rode.

It became increasingly clear as time went by that these Ton-Up boys represented a high-calibred section of British youth. They had all the qualities of nerve, intelligence, verve and leadership potential that a country would be only too grateful to exploit to the full in a time of war. But peacetime Britain has no idea of what to do with its young people. There is a mass of marvellous human material in this country simply going to waste.

Many of our Ton-Ups, during canteen discussions, spoke of emigrating. "This country is all washed up." But whether any of this particular group have suited action to their words I don't know.

One evening I made the foolish mistake of remarking that what they needed was virgin territory to explore. Howls of ecstasy greeted this. But their mirth was very good-natured and, after all, I had asked for it.

Lively, enthusiastic, dedicated, they crowded nightly into the canteen, their shiny red, black and white helmets and heavy dark gloves adorning the table-tops and canteen-counter, or stowed carefully away in corners. Outside stood parked the big, shiny bikes. The Ton-Ups talked, shouted, laughed, planned, drank coffees galore. The place was full to overflowing with them, the din of their voices together with the blare of the record-player was indescribable. Shortly before ten o'clock they donned their helmets and gloves, streamed out to the street, mounted their mechanized steeds and throbbed smoothly away into the night. An odd sense of combined adventure and nostalgia went with them.

Then, suddenly, they came to us no more. We were Out, another club or coffee-bar was In. No particular reason. Just the Ton-Up way.

PART TWO

LAISSEZ-FAIRE CLUB

"She's in that state of mind," said the White Queen, "that she wants to deny *something*—only she doesn't know what to deny!"

"A nasty, vicious temper," the Red Queen remarked; and then there was an uncomfortable silence for a minute or two.

Lewis Carroll
Through the Looking-Glass

CHAPTER VI

JINXED AGAIN

AT LAST IN early summer, our new full-time Leader arrived.
He was in his early twenties and extremely keen. He differed
entirely from his predecessor in approach, manner, appearance
and temperament. Brian had been slenderly handsome, a
Romantic in both physique and outlook, with a quiet, although
ready, sense of humour. He had been reflective, a little sardonic
in his private attitudes, and had distrusted gimmicks and
gadgets. Our new man was hefty, in appearance reminiscent
of a rugger-forward. He was given to loud, zesty whoops of
laughter and was all agog for the latest in ideas and objects.
He loved to be geared up.

He was a man who would go hiking on the South Downs
climbing-rope and karabiner-sling bedecked, hung around
with pitons, hammers and *étriers*, prepared for every eventuality
with compass, map, torch, adrenalin tablets, ciné-camera,
First Aid Kit, sun-tan lotion, anti-freeze lotion, water-purifying
tablets, anti-snake serum, midget transistor, binoculars, walkie-
talkie, tin-opener, bottle-opener, combined fork, knife and
spoon set, collapsible frying-pan and billy-can, drinking-cup
and water-flask, foldaway gas-stove, pocket-pack bivouac tent
with built-in sleeping-sack, instant potato, coffee, tea, milk;
dehydrated meat, soups, apples, bigos, goulash. Snow-goggles,
balaclava-helmet, swim-trunks, D.D.T. midge-repellant and
high-frequency whistle for calling-up lions.

He was generous, kind-hearted, impulsive. He liked to be
called Skipper, or Skip, as many Leaders do.

Inevitably a youth-club changes character with the appointment of a new Leader. With Skip at the helm we were clearly
going to attempt to be a "with it" Club ("with it" was still a
contemporary term). Skip felt most at ease amongst With It
young people from essentially middle-class backgrounds.
Coring-mushes whose coster-monger lineage had bequeathed
them raw-edged, tearing high-spirits that burst out in bouts of
fisticuffs or in "Knees Up Mother Brown" on pavements

63

outside pubs on a Friday night just weren't part of Skip's idiom. He did not speak their language, nor they his.

Thus many of our old, tough members left, including several of the weight-trainers. Among the girls who departed were Kat and Cleopatra. Kat thought the Club was going to turn "snobby". Cleopatra immensely disliked being asked to call the new man Skip. "More like a bleeding kipper." Neither did she like the way he spoke to the girls. "Rude perishing bugger. Shouts at you like you're a cocker-spaniel. No sodding manners at all." So exeunt Cleopatra, with a scornful flickering of her painted eye-lids.

I met her frequently thereafter while shopping in the town. She was working in a grocery-store. She never failed to ask after the Club's progress, accompanying her enquiries with uncomplimentary remarks about the unfortunate Skipper.

Rosebud also left. She was now in an advanced state of pregnancy and found coming to the Club embarrassing because "some of the new kids don't realize you're married, you know?"

Of course just as some members objected to Skip so did others warm to him.

During the Ton-Up regime the remaining original members (squares, Mids, incipient Mods, call them what you will) had either faded right into the Club background or had ceased to attend the Club at all. Now, with Skip as the Leader, they re-established themselves prominently.

The actual terms, Mod and Rock, did not come into active use until 1963, but the kids were naturally falling into Mod-Rock groups before that.

Rocks are the tough, rough, leather-jacketed, motor-bike mounted, overtly working-class, secondary-modern non-grammar-stream kids; the ones who never got the eleven-plus, the ones the grammar-stream kids call "thicks". Rocks like pop-music, bikes and tough gear (clothing). They join youth-clubs only so long as the club is strictly their sort of place. It mustn't be churchy, it mustn't be hearty, it mustn't be snobby or posh.

Mods are, very distinctly, not thick. Mods have passed the eleven-plus. Most of them come from homes which have achieved middle-class income level, though educational and even social status may lag some distance behind the family's material circumstances.

Mods delight in gimmicky possessions from midget transistors to karts. They conform scrupulously to the fashion trends in ideas as well as clothes. Formerly they rode scooters, today (1966) they have moved on to mini-cars. They never forget that they have their Joneses to keep up with. They care terribly about their image.

They are exceedingly contemptuous of Rocks. Rocks are socially and educationally inferior; in fact the equivalent of munts, in Mod eyes.

Rocks, not unnaturally, resent Mods. They resent them because they are snobby, superior, and the Rocks claim, soft. Most passionately of all the Rocks resent, god knows how deeply, the fact that Mods have been able to pass exams, are, in hateful contemporary idiom "bright".

The new class cleavage between the scholastically bright and not-so-bright is as bitter as any arising from purely economic distinctions. People who are bright at school look down their noses at the not-so-bright with undisguised contempt. The resentment and the basic sense of inferiority felt by young people who have failed to make the grade in this examination-ridden age can only be appreciated by persons who spend much time listening to teen-agers talking. The examination-failures believe themselves to be doomed. They are our contemporary sweeper-class, branded quite openly as inferior by the examination-passers, who refer to their non-academic contemporaries with an arrogance and sublime condescension which has to be heard to be believed.

Our Skip appealed to the Mod-style element at the Club rather than to the Rock mainly because, as Fred explained to me, he was more hot on the cultural side than the physical.

Several new members joined who naturally took their place in this budding Mod atmosphere. One of these was Hal, a tall, very argumentative boy who wrote television plays (that they were unaccepted doesn't really matter; he at any rate got them down on paper in their entirety, no mean feat in itself, as any writer knows). Hal was not only a playwright, he was also a football enthusiast. He planned to get together a football team.

He was, he told me, a retired Beatnik.

Beatniks are mainly drawn from young people in the late adolescent group and they are, of course, strictly unattached. Hal reminisced about his Beatnik days most interestingly:

"I was a Beat for about a year; then I'd had enough. It's

3

tough. To be a proper Beat you have to put your mind to it, go in for it dead serious. It's definitely not for weaklings, nor for kids. It's not for ordinary bums even, really. Like it's a genuine way of life; you could almost say you need a call to do it, like being a monk or something. You have to do it the whole hog; get dirty, grow your hair long, grow a beard. Some Beats sorta nibble at it, but it's no use being mish-mash about it. To be a topgrade Beat you got to get real way-out. It helps a hell of a lot with your prestige if you're a junky, or failing that develop a mania, or go schizo p'r'aps best of all. But I repeat, it's a life you can't keep up for long; not unless you got a will and a constitution of iron. Sooner or later you throw in the towel, stagger back home, fall on your little white bird, sorry I mean bed, and thank your lucky stars that your people are decent enough to welcome you back."

In spite of being more hot on the cultural side Skip was very keen on adventure groups, camping week-ends, and so on. But although he liked camping and camp-craft Skip was not a hearty, neither were his followers. Hearties are those keen, deeply committed, rather naïve, physical-fitness types one mainly meets in the uniformed youth-organizations. Boy Scouts, Girl Guides and their like are hearties (the Duke of Edinburgh Award Scheme unfortunately is associated in many minds with hearties, which is one of the reasons why it is so difficult to get young people from open youth-clubs to participate in the Scheme.)

Skip's attitude to Club activities was soundly geared to the tastes of contemporary moddy young people. His "cultural" interests and enthusiasms frightened off the toughs and thicks, but his idea of a club appealed very much to the other kids.

Our new Leader was soon asking for more money to be spent on the Club. He wanted more, and better, equipment. He demanded a telephone, a lounge in which members could be really comfortable and really relax, camping equipment, canoe-building gear, proper stage equipment, and so on.

All this was reasonable enough. The Club's financial position was by now considerably improved; our worst cheeseparing days were over, it seemed. The Albemarle Report had appeared and the Youth Service was beginning to lose some of its Cinderella features. The Authorities did not seem averse to at least a modest increase in Club expenditure. We now had a new Youth Officer (who had arrived in the town at the same time as Skip had joined our Club) and he pointed out to our Management Committee that the development of the Club must be our primary object. If this took more money then somehow the money must be found; we should apply for bigger local Authority grants and make more energetic fund-raising efforts of our own.

The Management Committee thereat made an application to the Education Authority for further grant-aid for equipment and furniture and also drew up an ambitious fund-raising programme with a target of a thousand pounds (which may not sound much to some people but was a sizeable sum for us to aim at). This programme included a circular letter of appeal, a stop-watch competition, carol-singing at Christmas, a bumper jumble-sale and a bazaar.

Word got around the town that we were intent on fund-raising and since the Youth Officer spoke warmly on our behalf to various people we soon had a very welcome donation of sports equipment from the Army and Quaker friends gave us a vaulting-horse.

Other philanthropic persons, hearing that we wanted furniture, off-loaded upon us a melancholy collection of geriatrics; upright pianos which were voiceless, scarred tables, an arthritic sideboard and several so-called easy chairs whose broken and oddly bulging springs made sitting upon them about as easy as reclining on the back of a dromedary.

Worn-out furniture and tatty old carpets should be burned or consigned to the refuse-collector, not given to youth-clubs.

The Management Committee pressed ahead with the installation of new heating. The old coke-stoves were removed and the Authority agreed to provide towards the cost of up-to-the-minute gas-radiators. But this was planning for winter, and so far as the members were concerned winter was far away. Their attention was engrossed with camping, swimming, holidays.

The Club entered for the local swimming-gala and did unexpectedly well; our team was captained by a new member named Chuck, who was an accomplished swimmer and diver. We didn't win the actual shield, but we did come second.

The kids also helped, enthusiastically, with a hospital garden-fête.

Fourteen boys who attempted an all-night walk to Southend (some fifty miles) did not make it, principally because the van which accompanied them to pick up stragglers proved too much of a temptation on the last half of the walk; they all became stragglers and boarded the van.

The Club closed for the month of August. Norine announced her resignation, for personal reasons. The members, who were very fond of her, organized a collection and raised such a generous sum that she was duly presented with an enormous bouquet of roses and a splendid box of chocolates. She stood in our tatty hall, holding the glossily beribboned, sumptuous roses and the extravagantly packed chocolates while the jean-and-T-shirted donors beamed proudly and tenderly at her. Tears blurred her last smiles. Then she was gone, driving down the dingy street in her little car, while everyone agreed that our next woman assistant Leader wouldn't never be as good as her.

Women assistant Leaders are hard to come by, whether good or mediocre. When the Club reopened in September we were still without a replacement for Norine, but we had found a male part-time assistant Leader; Timothy W., shy, sweet-natured and hard-working.

The promised new heating was not yet installed. The roof was still leaking badly; the builder, as usual, was said to have the matter in hand.

However, in spite of the leakage, the lounge had been redecorated by the members, ready for the new session. Different wallpapers and different shades of paint for each wall produced a most lively effect, contemporary curtains draped the windows and, the final touch, four diamond-shaped, blue-framed mirrors hung in a row on the longest, unbroken wall.

The decorators were excessively, indeed almost pathetically, proud of their efforts and received our compliments with broad, shy smiles. May the adult who loudly voiced disapproval condemning their taste, boil for eternity in a vat of scalding emulsion paint, stirred by demons chanting non-stop hit-parades.

Anyway, whatever the opinion of this one woefully vociferous person, the members themselves were thoroughly enchanted with the lounge and especially with the four mirrors, in front of which the boys nightly formed four little queues, taking it each in turn to comb their hair; each boy adapting an unvarying stance, feet braced apart, knees bent, body craned forward, left hand smoothing down the thick, longish (but not yet Beatle-long) hair while the right hand wielded the comb.

Only the boys used these mirrors; the girls never did so.

Skip had drawn up a promising winter-programme; road-safety talks, camp-craft, first-aid, film-making, motor-cycle rallies (to appease the toughs). Hal had formed his football-team; an aloof group of particularly large youths who favoured all-white as their team colour but changed to black-and-white as a concession to mud and laundry problems. Hal was their secretary and could be found, nightly, installed at the type-writer in the Leader's office, a frenetic two-fingered typist, either hammering out letters to rival secretaries in search of fixtures, or else working on one of his television dramas.

We now had exactly a hundred members; sixty-five boys, thirty-five girls. The Club could no longer really be described as a club for unclubables; our toughest element was composed of a small weight-training group and the footballers, none of whom, despite their toughness, might really be described as unclubable for they were, according to their own lights, a social-minded, enthusiastic lot, all interested in at least one definite Club activity, be it record-appreciation or football.

So we started to feel our way into a new sort of future.

A Hallowe'en Dance, at which hot fruit punch (non-alcoholic) and sausages were served while festooned turnip-lanterns grinned upon dancers capering demoniacally in a variety of spooky costumes (spooks, it seemed, did not jive cool) did much to set a promising seal upon our autumn session. But the dance was immediately followed by a chilling disaster. While dismantling the Hallowe'en decorations Skip fell from a step-ladder, sustaining injuries that put him out of action for the next three months. Our Club was jinxed again.

CHAPTER VII

GOD REST YOU MERRY, GENTLEMEN
–AND LADIES–
LET NOTHING YOU DISMAY

THE MANAGEMENT COMMITTEE found themselves once again called upon to staff a Leaderless club. There was no way out; the Club, like a show, had to go on.

The season of peace and goodwill was hard upon us and we had agreed to embark upon a week's carol-singing and house-to-house collections. I went round to the local police-station to obtain an application-form for a licence:

"In pursuance of Section 2 of the House to House Collections Act, 1939, I hereby apply for a licence authorizing me to promote the collection of which particulars are given below . . . "

The form ended with a stern warning in capital letters:

"NO PERSONS UNDER THE AGE OF 18 YEARS MAY ACT AS COLLECTORS."

"Make sure that only senior members take part in the collecting," said the Chairman, as he signed the application-form.

The Club members, on being asked to form carol-singing groups, declared as one that nothing on god's good earth would induce them to sing. We pleaded, cajoled; no use. They would not sing.

Finally it was decided to have a tape-recording of carols, with an amplifier, borne slowly round the streets on a float decorated with a fairy-lit tree. Accompanying the float would be parties of senior Club members, led by Lana dressed as Father Christmas; they would do the collecting. Each party of young people would be accompanied by an adult.

I did not at all like the suggestion of tape-recorded carols.

"Canned carols!" I said. "Oh God! Oh Montreal!"

"Are you prepared to sing?" enquired Mrs Z., briskly.

"No."

"Exactly what everyone says. So what's the alternative but a tape-recording?"

A friendly tradesman very sportingly offered to turn out nightly with his lorry, which would be used as the float. The members of the Management Committee each volunteered to put in an evening with the house-to-house collectors.

My evening came. It was a fine night, but dark.

I arrived at the Club to find Mrs Z. and the lorry-driver lashing the tree into position in the back of the lorry. The Treasurer was distributing collection-tins to the members.

"We'll send out two collecting parties tonight," said Mrs Z. "I'll take one lot in the mini-bus and you go in the lorry with the others. Some of the boys have their own transport; they'll follow the lorry. We'll do the Royal Drive Estate. My party to do all the roads off one side of the Drive, your party the other side. Dig?"

"Oughta get plenty of lolly up there," said Fred. "They're a posh lot up there."

The Treasurer handed me a tin. "Bring it back good and full," he said.

Each tin had a slot like a money-box in one end and a round hole in the other end. This hole, through which the money would in due course be extracted, was sealed by a paper-label.

I noticed Chuck quietly experimenting to see if he could remove the label on his tin.

He saw me watching his experiments with the label and flashed me an enchanting smile.

"Keep your hair on, lady. Just testing for security."

Lana came dancing up wearing an outsize Father Christmas suit, white beard and whiskers. "Crikey, it's hot in this outfit," she said.

"Bin down any chimneys yet, Lana?" asked Chuck. "Get your backside toasted."

"Don't put ideas into her head," said Clem. "Next we know she'll be wedged in a flipping chimney and Mrs B. will have to phone for the fire-brigade."

We were now ready to depart. Lana and I squeezed into the lorry-driver's cab; some of the other kids piled into the back of the lorry beside the Christmas tree, which now glowed with lights. Behind us came two small second-hand cars crammed with boys; Chuck drove one, Hal the other. Behind them came Mrs Z. in the loaded mini-bus and behind the mini-bus came a half-dozen or so motor-bikes. This convoy swung up the hill towards the Royal Drive Estate.

In the Drive itself, the major road of the estate, we stopped. As I climbed out of the lorry the amplifier began bellowing: "God rest you merry, gentlemen . . . " Lana skipped across the road waving her collecting-tin and singing, "Let nothing you dismay." A mob of boys, my party, chased after her. They started trying to pull her beard off. I tore after them, leaving Mrs Z. to her party and her side of the road. I could see that I had a frenzied evening ahead of me with the bunch I'd landed.

"Stop it, you lot. Don't forget that beard's stuck to her chin and if you pull it off it's a dead cert her head will come off with it!"

This made them laugh and they stopped tormenting Lana. They then began eyeing the neat, three-and-four bedroomed semi-detached houses which, they once again assured me, were the homes of the wealthy. For a moment the kids seemed intimidated at the thought of knocking on those orderly front-doors, almost every one of which had a porch-light shining above it. Clem said at last,

"Where'll we start, Mrs B?"

"Anywhere along here will do," I said.

"Orright, you lot," said Lana. "Let's start raking in the dosh."

Whereat their nerve and high-spirits returned to them magically and as one they each leapt forward flourishing a collecting-tin and lustily chanting, "Dosh! Dosh! Dosh!"

Keen as mustard we knocked on door after door, while the carols blared from the lorry in the roadway. Some people gave generously. Some gave frugally, but I at any rate encountered but one refusal. This was at a house where the door was opened by a pretty girl of about seventeen. I told her what I was collecting for and she called over her shoulder in the direction of the kitchen, "Mummy, there's a lady here collecting for a youth-club."

Mummy appeared from the kitchen. She looked decidedly unfriendly.

"A youth-club?"

"Yes," I said.

"Teen-agers?"

"Yes."

"I'm giving nothing to teen-agers. We don't believe in teen-agers here." And she popped back into the kitchen.

I looked enquiringly at her daughter. "What have you been doing?" I whispered. The girl gave me a huge shrug.

"Ah well, good luck," I said and turned away. I rejoined Lana and the boys.

"Draw a blank there?" asked Clem sympathetically. He went on, "How much you got so far?"

"About ten bob I should think."

"Old Chuck's got near on two quid."

"Two quid!"

"Must have," said Chuck complacently.

"One old bird just gave him ten bob," said Hal. "Must be his sexy good-looks."

"What's your technique, Chuck?" I asked.

"Simple," said Chuck. "I threaten 'em with my flick-knife. Say it's a stick-up."

"I'll have to get my knuckle-dusters and bicycle-chain out," said Lana. "Be a real teen-ager."

"Nice Father Christmas you are," said Hal. "What you put in the kiddies' stockings, pineapples?"

"If you really want to know how to get people to cough up, Mrs B.," said Chuck, drawing nearer to me and speaking confidentially, "it's this. Don't say you're collecting for a youth-club; that prejudices 'em from the start. Tell 'em like I do, collecting for the Mayor's Christmas Fund for deprived Children. They really go for that."

"But Chuck!" I was horrified. "That's false pretences!"

"No it ain't, 's good as the truth. All for the young, innit?"

"But Chuck, to mention the Mayor when he's got absolutely nothing to do with it . . . "

"Well, if he don't have a Christmas fund for children he bleeding well oughter," said Chuck.

Horrible visions of police-court appearances troubled me for the rest of the evening, in between bouts of laughter, for my companions were in tearing high spirits and the high spirits of the young are always infectious. At one point Hal who, in spite of his fondness for football, was a myopic and dreamy youth, missed a step in descending a garden-path, lurched, caught his toe in something, gave a cry, plunged wildly forward, struck his head against a porch-pillar and fell flat on his back as if pole-axed. There he lay while we, heaven help us, howled with mirth.

3*

"Bloody silly geezer, always falling over things," gasped Chuck at last. "Comes of being a highbrow. Never notices what he's doing."

The highbrow had meantime risen rather dazedly to his feet. I was afraid that he might be hurt, but now I heard him chuckling to himself.

He began groping his way back up the garden-path to us.

"Aren'tcha going to knock on the flipping door, arter all that?" shouted Fred.

"He thinks he has," said Henry. "Don't know where he is. A right nit."

"Didn't I knock on the door?" asked Hal. This reduced them all to tears of delight.

"Knocked on it with your bleeding nut, tosher," said Clem.

"Yeah, dives at the knocker head-first, old Hal do!"

"Yeah, bloke's a ruddy genius. Invents a new way of doin' everything!"

"We're making an awful row," I said. "There may be children asleep in some of these houses."

"Not now, Mrs B. We woke 'em all up."

"Come on, let's do another street," said Chuck. "Mrs B.'s right, these posh geezers don't like hooligans. We shan't get no more outa this lot 'cept dirty looks."

Accordingly we turned our attention to a crescent of detached houses. "Really in the lolly here, this lot," said Henry. "Whatsa betting they offer us a drink?"

"You're hopeful," said Fred. "Richer they are the meaner they get." A minute or so later Henry returned to my side, goggle-eyed and rather out of breath.

"'ere, Mrs B. See that house there, got a notice saying 'Christmas trees for sale'?"

"Yes, I saw that. Presumably he doesn't grow them himself."

"I don't know where he grows 'em, but he's bonkers."

"Bonkers?"

"Yeah. I knocked on the door, see? No answer. Knocked again, no answer. There was a light inside, so I knew someone was in. So I pushed open the letter-box and took a squint."

He paused. Clem, who was listening too, said, "Well, go on."

"There was stacks and stacks of trees, all stood round the hall, and in the middle of 'em a bloke jumping up and down, got no clothes on."

"Garn," said Clem. "You been drinking?"

"I tell you, there was this geezer in his birthday-suit dancing about 'mong a lot of flipping Christmas trees."

"Teach you not to look through letter-boxes," said Chuck.

"Cor, thank god I didn't ackchly knock. Suppose he'd opened the door? I reckon he was a maniac."

Clem waited until Henry had gone to another house, then he gave me a large wink. "Have to take old Henry's tales with a pinch of salt. Got a thing about maniacs, that bloke has. Always being chased by 'em."

The lorry had not followed us into the crescent and the strains of "While Shepherds Watched" were receding into the distance. I was anxious not to lose the lorry, or rather that it should not lose us, for the prospect of a long walk back to the Club was not entirely welcome after an evening of slogging up and down garden paths. After collecting from a few more houses I thought that perhaps I should round up my companions. It was now that I noticed that the street had suddenly grown very quiet. Where were my scurrying, laughing, box-rattling comrades? I was staring bemusedly about me when Henry appeared from behind the privet bushes of a bungalow.

"Obvious why old Chuck fetched us along this street, innit?"

"Why? Where have they all got to?"

"Nice little pub, just round the corner."

Lana hadn't gone into the pub; she was waiting for us by a lamp-post.

"Just like men, innit Mrs B.? They've all gone into the *Grapes* and left you and me to do all the work." She added, "We shan't see them again in a hurry."

Fortunately she was wrong. The boys soon came scuffling out of the pub, coshing one another playfully with their collecting-tins.

"Let's call it a day, eh, Mrs B?" said Hal. "My feet are pretty well worn out."

Everyone echoed this suggestion. We returned to the lorry. The driver too thought we should call it a day and switched off the tape-recording abruptly in the middle of, "Oh come ye, oh come ye to Bethle . . . " thus entirely destroying any shred of illusion that real carol-singers were out in the street.

Since Mrs Z. and her party had quite disappeared and since they were not relying upon us for transport we returned to the

Club, where the Treasurer was waiting to receive the tins, break open the seals and count the money. All the seals were perfectly intact. Everyone watched intently as the Treasurer shook on to the table the contents of tin after tin. Chuck's contribution evoked a cheer. He had two ten shilling notes and thirty-three shillings and sixpence in silver.

Our total takings amounted to seven pounds seven.

This was considered very good for one party and the Treasurer congratulated us. We then went into the canteen and warmed ourselves with coffee.

"See what I mean, Mrs B.?" said Chuck. "If the whole lot of you had collected for the Mayor's Fund, same as me, we'da done even better."

As he spoke Mrs Z. bundled in, surrounded by a tin-waving group of considerably younger members. "How much you get?" they bawled at us.

"Seven quid. Seven quid and seven bob. How much you get?"

These younger kids started shoving their tins at the Treasurer who stood opening tins and counting money frantically. Mrs Z. said to me sharply, "What's that about the Mayor's Fund?"

"Old Chuck got over two quid on his jack, saying it was for the Mayor's Fund," said Fred.

Mrs Z. was appalled. She looked at me with a reproach too acute for words. Finally she managed to exclaim, "But Mary! How could you allow . . . " I, meantime, had been fumbling in my handbag. I took out a crumpled piece of paper, unfolded it, handed it to her, cutting her short.

"Read what it says in capital letters at the bottom," I said.

Slowly she read aloud, "No persons under the age of eighteen years may act as collectors."

"Your lot all eighteen?" I asked her sweetly.

Everyone started to roar.

She turned huge, horrified eyes to mine. "But nobody ever told me a word of that before!"

Then, to do her credit, she began laughing as loudly as the rest of us. Finally she said, "It's dreadful, though. I mean we could all land up in court."

"All spend Christmas in the cooler," said Chuck.

The carol-singing realized a total sum of twenty-five pounds; not at all bad, really.

On December 23rd the Members' Committee laid on a party

with a buffet, dancing to a local group of repute, and spot-prizes. The lights were dimmed in the big hall and here the members jived with unusual animation, boys actually partnering girls in some daring instances. The Management Committee were regaled with coffee, sausages and mince-pies. I was on duty in the canteen with Katina. She served refreshments while I did the washing-up. Katina adored serving refreshments. As she served she talked to me. Rosebud, she said, had had her baby, ever such a lovely little boy. He was going to be called Christopher Stephen. Rosebud had had a very easy time, but the hospital sister made her cut all her long finger-nails off before she would let her bath the baby. Cleopatra and Katina had visited Rosebud in hospital and had taken her a pot of white heather and some chocolates.

"What about the layette you were making for her?"

"Oh, we give her that four weeks ago, in case the little kid arrived early. You should see what she had in it; smashing it was. Her mum wouldn't believe we'd done it all ourselves. Old Cleo nearly knitted her fingers off; she finished up doing a whacking big shawl, all with fancy fringe, you know. But the mitts wasn't too good. They turned out ever such a funny shape, more like bootees, you know?"

Presently Kat asked if she could leave me to cope alone as she wanted to dance, and soon I noticed her jiving with Chuck. He used what I called the hurdy-gurdy technique, grasping her hand and turning it mechanically as if he were an organ-grinder, while she spun jerkily round and round, her expression utterly dead. Nevertheless it was apparently pleasurable to them both, for they did it all the rest of the evening.

Indeed the party was immensely enjoyed by everyone except poor Henry. He had ordered a new suit to be made for the occasion, but the tailor had succeeded only in completing the trousers in time. Henry, wearing these trousers, highly-polished stacked-heeled boots, a dazzling new white shirt and a narrow red silk tie, his hair coiffured meticulously, hid himself in the Leader's office. There he remained all evening, purple-faced with disappointment and mortification, refusing to accept innumerable assurances that he looked smashing as he was, without a jacket. Every now and again we glimpsed him peering round the partly opened door, watching everyone else having a wonderful time.

CHAPTER VIII

LAISSEZ-FAIRE

THE WARM GENIALITY of Christmas evaporated into the biting winds of January and still Skip remained out of action.

It is a fact, of course, that all youth-workers, however keen, confess to periods of defeatism and despondency. Most of our Management Committee were by now in one of these disenchanted moods. If anyone had asked them how they liked young people they would have replied, in the style of W. C. Fields, "Parboiled."

At last Skip returned. He had obviously been doing a lot of thinking and planning. It was clear that, whereas before his accident he had been rather cautiously feeling his way with his new Club, he now believed that the time had come to put into practice all the theories that he so ardently entertained.

These all verged towards a permissive-style club: experience had not yet hardened Skip's approach. An understanding Management Committee might have guided him away from the major pitfalls of permissivity while at the same time sympathetically assisting him to try out some of his undeniably good schemes. But our Management Committee was undergoing what might be termed an anti-youth reaction. Conflict between Committee and Leader was therefore ultimately inevitable.

Skip's programme of activities for the coming months included record appreciation, tape-recording sessions, a cinema-club, impromptu drama, readings of Pinter and of *Under Milk Wood*, photography and a wall-newspaper. Photography fell flat, while the wall-newspaper seemed to be exclusively the work of Hal and of Skip himself. But the impromptu drama and the taping sessions went very well, *The Caretaker* and *Under Milk Wood* catching on surprisingly. Record appreciation also prospered; the records were mainly trad jazz, Peter Sellers, Spike Milligan and the ever-to-be-lamented Hoffnung.

Mrs Z., who felt that record-appreciation should be directed towards what she called classical music, rather than Peter

78

Sellers, brought down some records of Tchaikowsky's "Casse Noisette" one evening. These she put on to play, without comment. We waited to see what happened. Nobody took any notice at all. At last one boy, drinking cokes in the canteen with his mate, said, "Whassat?"

"What's what?" said the mate.

"That music."

The pal listened a moment, then said, obviously rather pleased with himself for knowing, "I think it's called 'The Dance of The Sugar Plum' or something."

"Gergh," said the other derisively, "next you'll be saying it's the waltz of the flippin' Candy Floss."

That was all the appreciation Tchaikowsky got.

Another Skip experiment (Mrs Z. didn't attempt any more) was mock trials, but these were limited in scope because the only trials the kids were interested in were murder trials.

Skip now decided to promote one or two senior members to the status of helpers. Helpers enjoyed privileges such as paying no subs, free entry to dances, and so on. Chuck, Clem and Fred became helpers. So far so good; then Skip began to select trusties who greatly alarmed the Cubes on the Management Committee. Slim, just out of an approved school, was quiet, with an undertone of viciousness; his eyes held an oddly blank, slightly stunned expression. He had a wretched home background. Skip made him a helper in the hope that responsibility would develop the boy. "He's a helper orright; helps himself left, right and centre to everything going in the canteen," said the Treasurer, when the question of Slim came up for discussion. Mr N. leapt forward in defence of the boy. "Give the poor little blighter a chance. He's not that bad; given a break he might very well make good."

But even Mr N. quailed before Skip's next addition to the list of helpers. This was a youth whom the Treasurer dubbed at first sight "Young Lochinvar". We shortened this to Lock. Young Lochinvar, it will be remembered, came out of the West and if this bold youth of ours didn't in fact come out of the West he certainly looked as if he did. His sideburns, neckerchief, checked shirt and skin-tight jeans tucked into cowboy boots were all undeniably Western. Especially the boots. They made one immediately look for a lariat.

He was noisy and brash, self-confident (at least outwardly)

and a non-stop talker. His features were sharp and his leer broad and knowing; if he had worn a cat's skin cap, and caulkers instead of boots, he would have looked remarkably reminiscent of the imperishable Mr William Hare of Tanner's Close, Edinburgh. But it was not upon Hare that Lock modelled himself; his hero was a more recent villain, Al Capone.

Of Capone and his exploits Lock talked endlessly while the other Club members listened; at first fascinated, then with increasing boredom, until at last they drifted away muttering, "That poor bloke's off his nut."

Lock's theme was that he was going to be a second Al Capone, only a very much bigger one. "Make a fortune first, see, cornering the market in drugs and women. Then I'm gonna take over."

"Take over what?"

"Everything. Blooming universe."

"You lack ambition mate. That's your trouble."

"Give me seven years, an' you'll see. I'll be a bigger dictator than Hitler."

And so on, as he stood behind the canteen-counter, serving cokes and crisps.

Skip was sorry for the youth and again thought that responsibility might be therapeutic.

What with Hal's dramatic group intoning choice extracts from *The Caretaker*, the non-stop playing of Peter Sellers' unforgettable chanting of *You Are The Promised Kiss of Springtime* (a record surely appreciated by all right-minded persons), Lock extolling Al Capone, and Slim helping himself to choc bars with accomplished sleight of hand, the Management Committee had a lot of adjusting to do.

Red now returned. Apparently he had heard that our old place was looking up. He sported a new hair-style, known as the "angel-cut", and wore a sleeveless coon-skin jacket. He looked like a Giotto friar out of Davy Crockett. His friar-like appearance was heightened by the fact that, whenever possible, he went about barefoot. It transpired that his current girlfriend was a Raver and he was much under her influence. A small coterie of Red adherents sprang up who removed their shoes upon entering the Club in the manner of Muslems entering a mosque.

Our Club membership now stood at seventy-eight; forty-one boys, thirty-seven girls. This was an unusually high proportion of girls; yet, when a new Members' Committee was formed, only three girls could be persuaded to sit upon it.

The average age of the girls was lower than it had been in the past. The little creatures were all very heavily made-up, especially about the eyes, while their stiffly lacquered, back-brushed hair styles were wonderful to see.

And now Cleopatra returned, unofficially engaged to one of Hal's cronies. With her came Rosebud and her husband Howard. The first evening they brought the baby in its pram; Cleopatra, who was the child's godmother, was almost as proud of him as Rosebud was. "Smashing little bugger, isn't he?"

We all crowded around, admiring the infant, who was fat, happy and spotlessly clean. But this was his only Club appearance; thereafter he was left with Rosebud's mother.

Among other faces that now reappeared was the serene visage of Rory, apparently a reformed character. He sat quietly in the canteen every evening, looking angelic. But his week-ends were spent otherwise; within a few weeks of regaining his freedom he went inside again, Borstal this time, for assaulting coppers in places as far apart as Brighton and Walthamstow.

So the year advanced. Daffodils, tulips and lilacs succeeded one another. Skip's adventure groups journeyed, rope bewound, karabiner-beslung and rucksack burdened into the heart of wildest Sussex. Somebody broke an electric-light fixture trying to rappel from a beam at the Club. The Management Committee spoke warningly about injuries and insurance. Hal sent his play to A.T.V. and got it back; he was much dejected, but I revived him with the story of a (now successful) writer of my acquaintance who, in his early days, had received enough rejection-slips to paper a loo in Clerkenwell. Hal at once started another play.

Cleopatra organized a week-end at Herne Bay. The drama group read *A Taste of Honey*.

The Club, although only on the small side now, so far as membership went, was active enough, noisy enough, lively enough, but it had an extraordinary helter-skelter, hither-and-thither quality about it. Somehow it made one think of a handful of confetti tossed into the air to twirl on the wind; nothing seemed definite, nothing was cohesive. Episodes, conversations flowed into one another, so that at one moment you were discussing hiring a bell-tent for a week-end of camping and boating and then, when you got the bill, it was for thirty yards of maroon-coloured hessian for a curtain at the back of a portable apron-stage. In fact, before long the Club, for me at all events, began to resemble Alice's adventures through the looking-glass, with Skip, round-headed, round-eyed, wide-mouthed and giant school-boyish as he was, like Tweedledum or, contrariwise, Tweedledee. When one walked past the chipped plaster spastic child down the narrow street of little houses and entered the Club by a small door set within a large door, one stepped into the world of Jabberwocky and found that,

> "Twas brillig, and the slithy toves
> Did gyre and gimble in the wabe:
> All mimsy were the borogroves,
> And the mome raths outgabe."

Still, it seemed to be working, and that was all that really mattered.

Then, suddenly, a new open-club arrived, only a few streets away. This club had a live pop-group of its own and our members, including Cleopatra, Rosebud and Howard, Chuck, Red, Clem, Henry and all the little doe-eyed, bee-hived, winklepickered girls left in one fell-swoop, lured away by the sound of this group.

Only Fred, the frenetically play-scribbling Hal and dear Lana, Lock and a few of the weight-trainers remained with us.

This dire drop in members meant, too, a drop in our income from subscriptions and canteen-takings. We seemed to be heading for disaster, quickly.

During this period of crisis we had a change of Management Committee officers. Both the Chairman and the Vice Chairman stood down from office under pressure of other commitments.

Nobody wished to take the chair in place of the outgoing Chairman. The Youth Officer referred to the chair jokingly (possibly not very originally) as "the hot seat", but in our Club it really was a hot spot to occupy and understandably nobody rushed forward to be seated in it. Finally, to my genuine amazement and considerable reluctance, I found myself installed upon it, with everyone else grinning with relief to find that they were not.

It looked rather as if my first function, on becoming Chairman, would be to wind up the Club, but then, absolutely out of the blue, the Corporation made us a grant of a hundred pounds. This was pure manna. Financially, at least, we could now carry on for a bit longer.

But what about members? They were all clapping and stamping to the strains of the pop-group round the corner.

Then came the annual local swimming-gala. A large contingent of erstwhile members, headed by Chuck, presented themselves to swim for our Club. Although scarcely a soul in this team was in fact a paid-up Club member (properly speaking all were members of the rival club, which would undoubtedly have disqualified the team had the matter reached the ears of the judges) our Club triumphantly bore off the gala trophy; a large shield which was mounted on our canteen wall.

"An expression of Club loyalty," explained Chuck.

During the actual gala I sat in the gallery of the Number One bath with Rosebud and Cleopatra on either side of me (Howard and Cleo's unofficial fiancé were swimming) and we cheered ourselves blue in the face during every event for which our team entered.

But immediately the gala was over every one of the kids returned to the rival club.

It all felt more like *Through The Looking Glass* than ever. Our loyal members were *not* our members, while three of the most devoted of these most devoted youth-club non-members were a married couple and the godmother of their child.

And the shield of victory which glittered in our canteen had no right to be there and we had no right whatever to be proud of it.

Poor Mrs Z., serving coffees, rolled her eyes up at the shield. "We call this social work, but sometimes you know I really do feel it's more like we do anti-social work. I mean, we encourage these kids down here to do things like this shield, and the time we went carol-singing."

"The main thing for social-working ladies like yourselves is not to get your collars felt," said Lock. "So long as you don't actually end up in the nick you're orright."

The Club closed for a long summer recess that year; we all felt that we needed a good breather. When we opened again in the second week of September we were still small numerically, no more than forty-two members; thirty-one boys and eleven girls. Many of these were absolutely new members, although Lana was still with us, and so were Fred, Lock and Hal, and the stalwarts of the football team.

The team's first game of the season resulted in a sweeping victory.

The players were, as I have said, all very large; more like a rugger than a soccer side, and they were exceedingly tough. Tough, indeed, in every sense of the word. They had quickly gained a reputation as a very dirty side and the threat of disqualification hung over them constantly. Of this they were unabashedly proud. An ingenious foul by one of the team roused intense admiration in the rest, who did their best to follow suit with a succession of even more ingenious fouls. A sporting spirit, in the conventionally understood sense, seemed wholly lacking. Skip unwisely filmed the highlights of some of their games and showed this film to the Management Committee. Comment was adverse.

Nevertheless it *was* a team and it *did* turn out regularly. We had never managed to produce a football team at all, hitherto; there had been much talk of one, but never any do. Therefore I urged that this team was, in its own peculiar fashion, something of which we might feel quite proud. But I could find few to agree with me.

Meanwhile we had finally got a new woman part-time assistant Leader; Mrs Bonny C., youthfully middle-aged and sweet. Under her guidance the girls did sewing and handicrafts; the sewing-machine was an old treadle one which appealed enormously to several of the younger boys who, given a chance, sat treadling and stitching to distraction while the girls complained that they had no chance to do any sewing.

The girls, like our previous intake, were on the junior side and all very painted, especially round the eyes. They fluttered cerulean-blue lids circled smudgily with green; some experimented with black, violet and blue blended, so that they appeared to have met with the famous Cockney mishap of "walking into a bird-cage in the dark" (having been punched in the eye by one's old man, or old woman).

Two girls in particular, Dee and Dolly, appeared with spectacular eye effects. Dee, small, skinny, electric, hard-faced, *jolie-laide*, fifteen but sometimes looking nearer fifty, was all gleaming teeth, green eyelids with silver highlights, and white, tight sweaters. She could behave charmingly when she chose, but she could also be a little devil, with an even worse vocabulary than Cleopatra's. Her mate, Dolly, was plump and bovine, with a mass of hair lacquered upright like *Struwwelpeter* of nursery memory; her eyes grew nightly blacker and greener and bluer and her high-pitched giggle was all nit-wit provocation. Both girls were very boy conscious.

Each slapped about in slingback sandals and each carried a wicker hen-basket into which they crammed scarves, spare cardigans, nylons, sweets, knitting, cigarettes, lighters, lacquer hair-sprays, hair-rollers, make-up, nail-varnish, varnish remover, cotton-wool, scissors, nail-files, letters from boys, address books, brushes, combs, dressing-mirrors, and heaven only knows what else.

We seemed, too, to have some very little boys about the place; these sky-larked around keeping up a high-pitched clamour of sound like starlings at sunset. A pair of these (just fifteen and left school, but looking more like thirteen) became very friendly with me. Named Midge and Gavin respectively they chain-smoked like veterans and were always together, sharing their cash, cigarettes and adventures. They expressed stirringly loyal sentiments towards the Club. "Best bloody youth-club round here, mate." They addressed everyone as mate.

One evening Midge arrived with his arm heavily bandaged and in a sling. He was accompanied, of course, by the inevitable Gavin. I asked Midge what he had done to his arm.

"Fell off the back of a park seat, mate."

"How on earth d'you do that?"

"Why, me an' my mate here, we was being circuses on this seat, see, an' I was doing a tightrope act along the bleeding back of it an' fell off."

"Good heavens."

"Ger, that's nothin'. Nothin' for me, is it mate?" said Midge to Gavin.

"No, nothin' for him," said the faithful Gavin. "I tell you, mate, this bloke here's had more accidents than any other livin' geezer his age. This bloke here'll never die in his bed, that's for sure."

Midge laughed happily. "No, never die in my bed."

"What sort of accidents?" I asked.

"Cor, some real good 'uns," said Gavin. "Nearly bin drowned, my mate has . . . "

"Nearly bin run over, but that was when you wasn't there, Gav."

"Nearly fell off the roof at the cinema."

"Good grief. How?"

"Climbed up on the roof, we did," said Gavin. "During one of them Sat'day mornin' shows for little'uns. This was when we was young."

"Got up on the roof through a trap-door," said Midge. "Walked over the roof, like, and come to a parapet, you know?"

"My mate here," said Gavin, "went to look over the bleedin' parapet an' he slipped. Don't know how he done it, but he slipped over the flippin' edge." He started to laugh at the memory of it. Midge began laughing too.

"Don't know how I slipped, but blimey, I went. Nearly fell clean off into the bleedin' street below, but somehow I sorta hooked myself up by me elbows as I was goin', an' that saved me. Everythin' miles down below, all the traffic an' everythin'. I thought I'd had it, straight, 'cos I couldn't hang there by my elbows for ever."

"What did you do?"

"I said to my mate here, 'Do something, you silly sod, 'steada laughing.' So he ran and fetched the manager. And he yanked me back. I couldn't've hung on much longer."

"He was about sixty feet up," said Gavin.

"Eighty more like it," said Midge. "Bleedin' long way to drop."

"We didn't half laugh arterwards though," said Gavin. "My mate, hangin' there, purple in the face, staring at me over the wrong side of the parapet and sayin' 'Do something.' "

"What did the manager say to you?"

"Oh, he was proper shook, mate. Too blooming shook to say nothing. Went white as a sheet. We thought he was gonna faint."

Pause while they ordered two more coffees.

"Funniest time though was when I nearly got drowned," said Midge.

"Cor, that was ripe, mate," said Gavin.

"Me an' my mate 'ere, we went to spend a day by the river. At the weir there they got one of them there booms, it lies just under the top of the water, like, so you can't see it, but it's there alla same. Well, I climbed on to this boom and walked along it. You couldn't see I was walkin' on anything, looked jus' like I was walkin' on the water."

"Looked jus' like he was walkin on the bleeding water."

"An' I was waving my arms and shouting, 'Look at me, I'm Jesus Christ walking on the water. Look at Jesus Christ walking on the water!' And then, alla sudden, I slipped an' fell in."

"He can't swim, my mate can't."

"So I started to drown. I could feel meself drownin'. Coo, it was perishin' 'orrible. And then the ole lock-keeper come running an' he pulled me out. Took me to his little house by the lock and dried all me clothes for me an' give me dinner an' then sent me home. A real decent old bloke."

"My mate's Mum, though, she half murdered him when he got home."

"Yeah. I told her I bin playin' at Jesus Christ and she said, 'I'll teach you to play bloody daft games like that!' "

More fits of laughter.

"Looked jus' like Jesus Christ though, didn't I mate?"

"You bleedin' did an' all, mate, till you fell in."

"Break my neck yet," said Midge.

"Live in hope," said Gavin.

I then related to them the story of how I once broke my neck. To this unlikely, but in fact authentic, tale they listened entranced.

"And you're still alive?" said Midge.

"No," I said. "I'm a top-grade embalming job."

After this session we were buddies for life.

The financial position of the Club, although vastly improved thanks to the Corporation grant, still required careful watching. We were still on the 7 p.m. to 7 a.m. electricity tariff, which Skip found very inconvenient now that the days were drawing in, but the Treasurer insisted that we must remain on it for purposes of economy.

It was decided to boost our bank balance with a giant jumble-sale. We had printed a great batch of leaflets announcing the sale and asking for jumble. These were to be distributed by the Club members from house to house, over the district, a fortnight before the sale, to be followed up by van-borne teams collecting the jumble itself.

The first hitch occurred when most of the Club members refused to distribute leaflets.

The second appeared in the mysterious guise of a young man of short, slight build (we were told) who said that he had come to collect jumble for our Club and who then made off with a sizeable amount of the stuff which helpful householders (those to whom leaflets had been distributed, mainly by Mrs Z., myself, and Lock) had put out ready for us. Naturally we never saw any of the stuff; neither did we ever identify the young man, although Mrs Z. and I each nursed dark suspicions.

The official jumble-collecting parties proved difficult to organize; most of the kids still refused to co-operate.

On the evening I went out to collect jumble my party consisted of a respectable tradesman who had offered both his van and himself to drive it (I must say here that several local business people were very kind in helping us in this way; I only regret that some of them found the experience rather trying), Midge, Gavin and Hal, and myself. The two little boys were there to fetch the jumble from the houses. Hal had the job of stacking it in the van, while I was supposed to supervise the exercise in general.

So far as I am concerned running a jumble-sale is always an unmitigated pleasure. I adore, shamelessly, all kinds of junk. White-elephant stalls, flea markets, rubbish-dumps fascinate me. As for a jumble sale, why you never know what you are going to find amongst the jumble!

It was therefore with a real sense of delicious adventure that I set out that evening. I quickly discovered that Hal, too, was a jumble-fiend.

Skip handed me a piece of paper as we were about to start. "Here's the addresses you're to call at."

"Posh part of the town, eh, tonight?" said Midge, as we drove off, leaving Skip gesturing a sort of "Good luck and good hunting" signal from the pavement.

"We oughta get some nice things," said Gavin.

"Old antiques," said Hal. "Worth having. Last night we got some crumby stuff."

We chattered about marvellous objects that sometimes turn up amongst jumble; old pieces of porcelain worth hundreds of pounds, old first-editions worth thousands.

Finally we drew up at our first port of call. Gavin and Midge darted off up a small driveway and quickly reappeared hauling between them, with difficulty, a small, tatty chest-of-drawers. Hal helped them get it into the van. Its drawers were stuffed with apparent rubbish.

The boys started pulling everything from the drawers as the van travelled further along the street. Our driver said, "Don't start to unpack yet, lads. We don't want any of the stuff unpacked at this stage. Don't unpack etc etc." But Hal, Midge and Gavin paid no heed and I simply could not resist slewing round in my seat beside the driver and watching what they brought out of the drawers.

"Old specs . . . rags . . . old knives an' forks . . . No sodding first editions here, mate. Cor, look at this awful old pair of pants! Blimey, what's this I got? Old picture of a spotty old geezer . . . "

"That's all mildew, them spots."

"Won't fetch nothing, that."

"See what's in that bottom drawer."

"Cor!"

"Cor, look at this! Cor mate! Fab!"

"Blimey, they're worth something. Look at these, Mrs B. I say, d'you think they're Ming?"

I inspected the two oriental-style vases that Hal was holding. The little boys breathed hard with excitement.

"Mate, they're luscious."

"Mate, they're worth a bomb."

"Sell 'em to me, Mrs B.?" asked Hal.

"No."

"Give you ten bob."

"You put them safely back into that drawer. No buying or selling until the real sale starts on Saturday."

"Ten bob each."

"Put 'em back in the drawer."

Hal put the vases carefully back in the drawer. "Wouldn't surprise me at all if they was Ming," he said. "That's how these things turn up."

Our driver obviously did not like jumble; he didn't even so much as glance at the vases. Neither did he much like our Club members. He had, he said, as we drew up at the next address on my list, no time for the young ones of today. I wondered why the hell he had offered to help us.

The little boys ran from house to house, staggering back with armfuls of stuff; old books, lamp-shades, tatty clothing, rattling radio-sets, cracked china, dusty picture-frames, broken tennis-racquets and so forth. They chattered like magpies while Hal and I inspected the stuff and stowed it in the van. Then we drove on again, the boys constantly dropping off to call at houses.

I commented upon their agility as they leapt from the moving van, chased it, boarded it, hopped off again. Midge said, "Ger, this is nothin' mate. We're paper-boys, me an' my mate here. Go round with the *News* van, evenings. We really get bombing then, don't we Gav?"

"Not half," said Gavin. "My mate here, he can jump offa van what's doing forty."

"Go on with you," said our driver.

"Straight he can, guv. Old Midge he can jump offa van doing forty, dead easy."

"Don't tell me," said the driver.

"Orright mate, just you accelerate an' my mate here will show you."

The driver grinned derisively and trickled on at the same pace as before.

"Go on mate, step on it," urged Gavin. "You think I'm lying, doancher?"

"Cut it out," said the driver. "We're on serious business tonight, not playing fun and games."

"My mate here, he can chase a van what's doin' thirty," declared Gavin.

The driver laughed loudly. So did Hal.

"Last night when we was out collectin' jumble with that old Treasurer bloke my mate got left behind by his van and so my mate put on a spurt; cor, you shoulda see 'im. Pretty near doin' forty, old Midge was, last night."

"Better put himself forward for Tokyo," said the driver.

"You was near doing forty last night, wasn't you Midge?"

Midge laughed modestly. "I was going pretty fast."

"I looked out an' saw him . . . cor, blurred he was," said Gavin.

From the next house the boys returned with a lot of books through which Hal rummaged for science-fiction. Meantime Midge and Gavin tried another house and were rewarded with bales of stuff. They lugged it to the van, calling loudly, "Here, look what we got for you, Mrs B.! Smashing tweed suit!"

"Good lord!" muttered the driver.

Midge put his head in at the window next to me. "Jus' what you want for Scotland. Skirt's got pleats for walkin', and two pockets, one for your map an' one for your compass."

"Try her with this hat!" shouted Gavin. He came scampering to the van. "See what you look like in this hat, mate."

Gavin pressed on to my head a yellow boat-shaped straw with roses. Midge, who was trying to display to me the beauties of the suit, climbed beside Gavin. They wound their arms round my neck lovingly and stared intently at me as I sat behatted. "It don't suit you . . . *Not* your style, mate, not-at-all."

They whisked the hat off me, then began showing me the suit. A woman had come from the house from which the boys had fetched these things; she stood watching us with interest.

The driver was horribly embarrassed. "People will think we're collecting this stuff for ourselves."

I was laughing. He turned to me all angry indignation. "I don't want people to think I rig myself out in second-hand clothes," he said.

I could see that the evening was turning out to be a bad experience for him.

Our van continued on its round, with Midge and Gavin bouncing, running, slamming the van doors, crashing gates, knocking knockers, shouting in glee when something good turned up. Hal in his turn kept up a running commentary on the swag, as he called it. I laughed. The driver suffered.

"We'll wake the neighbourhood. Mark my words, Mrs B., there'll be complaints over this."

"Heavens, it's not that late," I said. "Only just on eight. People surely don't go to bed at this hour."

"We sound like a travelling-circus."

"Go down Grove Gardens, guv," urged Midge. "Old bird down there's promised to dig out a railway-guard's uniform, complete. Skip says I can keep the cap."

The boy repeated this request several times and finally to Grove Gardens we went. Midge scuttled up to a corner house and presently back he came, a grotesque little dancing figure in a guard's coat that reached down well below his knees. "Stand clear of the doors! Stand clear of the doors!" He signalled with an imaginary flag, gave a piercing whistle, then started to chuff and stamp. Our driver watched this performance in agony. Hal and Gavin cheered.

"Wheresa bleeding cap, mate?" asked Gavin at last, leaning out of the van window as Midge chuffed and stamped up to us.

"She couldn't find it. Says if I come back Friday she'll take another look. Smashing old coat though, innit?"

We left Grove Gardens for a neighbouring crescent; here we got some things from people our driver knew. He urgently requested the boys to quieten down as we drove along here. "We're not a Karno troupe, you know. This is a first-rate residential area where I'm well known."

So along this first-rate residential street we drove sedately; the lads behaving quietly and beautifully. Several donors of jumble exchanged courtesies with our driver who beamed and cast me sidelong glances of triumph. I was happy for him; he had had such a wretched evening so far, while I on the contrary had thoroughly enjoyed myself.

From this street we got a standard-lamp, some toddlers' toys, chintz curtains and matching cushion covers, a parcel of ancient and extremely heavy venetian-blinds and a dog's collar and lead.

Finally the owner of an elegant white bungalow informed us that he had some shoes for us. Midge went into the bungalow to collect the shoes; meantime Gavin remained in the van, arguing that he should be entitled to the dog's collar and lead since Midge was getting the guard's cap. Then I saw Midge emerge from the bungalow, carrying several pairs of shoes. The owner watched from his doorstep, vastly amused, as Midge, waving one particular pair in triumph, raced up the road to our van bawling at the top of his voice to the driver,

"Guv, guv, what size shoes you take? I got a smashing pair here, good as new, do you lovely if they fit!"

Poor driver! This was really the final straw. He was humiliated beyond words. Brusquely he refused to collect any more jumble and drove us back to the Club.

My personal moment of horror came about half-an-hour later when some of the senior boys who had also been jumble-collecting returned with several well-filled P.D.S.A. collection sacks.

"But you shouldn't have brought those sacks back here," I said. "They aren't intended for us."

"Jumble, lady, belongs to them what collects it," said Lock.

"That jumble," I said, "was put out for the P.D.S.A., not for us."

"Don't panic, Mrs B.," said Chuck (he had now returned to our fold from the rival club round the corner). "All's fair in love and war, innit? This jumble-sale lark's a war, innit? We whip theirs, they whip ours."

"You must take it back."

"Stone it, Mrs B., how we to remember which perishin' door-steps we knocked it off?"

"These people thought their jumble was gonna help little bow-wows. Well, instead it's gonna help us."

"Youth's more deservin' than dogs, innit?"

I gave up. I was out-talked and out-numbered.

The actual sale itself went pretty well, considering that we had not got very much jumble to sell, in spite of the P.D.S.A. haul. We sold everything but the virtually unsaleable. We left Lock to negotiate the removal of this debris by a seedy-looking individual who dealt in rags, old lumber and heaven knows what else and who was, Midge assured me, a millionaire. While Lock and the millionaire haggled over some bits of carpet the rest of us squeezed into Skip's office where the Treasurer was counting the money we had taken.

"Scouts got over a hundred quid, their last jumble-sale," Gavin kept saying.

We had made just over fifteen pounds.

The Management Committee felt that we had not been more successful with the sale because of lack of effort on the part of the Club members due to lack of drive on the part of Skip. He should have *made* the members collect more jumble, said his critics. Skip's reply was that one should never *make* young people do anything. They should, he said, only do what they themselves wish to do. Left to their own inclinations and spontaneous impetus they will do what really interests them and do it with the maximum of effort and the minimum of tension.

Coercion makes them tense, unco-operative and finally aggressive.

That this *laissez-faire* approach to youth-club work did not succeed in practice, however attractive it might sound in theory, became duly apparent at the Club. The place became increasingly chaotic. Many of the quieter members began to drop away, leaving only the very noisy, uncontrolled ones. The ebullience of such youngsters as Midge and Gavin grew more and more exaggerated, until it reached a point where it was positively disruptive. Furthermore tension and aggression, those two moods which Skip's *laissez-faire* methods were supposed to avoid, appeared very definitely. The members, allowed their own way in everything, had reached that stage where they longed, in their hearts, to have something to knock up against. So they shouted, barged, bashed, crashed and smashed; snarled "no" where formerly they would have smiled "yes", and appeared as unpleasant, unfriendly, downright nasty little creatures.

Any kind of organized activity was impossible with them when they were in that mood. So they banged and crashed and slouched and swore while a tight little nucleus of older members formed itself round Skip and indulged in activities of an increasingly coterie nature; an In-Group. This In-Group was, of course, resented by the other members, who became, as a result, even more unpleasant and aggressive.

No, laissez-faire did *not* work.

CHAPTER IX

ANTI-SOCIAL INTERLUDES

LOCK'S PLANS FOR world domination now extended themselves from cornering the international market in whores and drugs to liquidating what Hitler had left of the Jews. He claimed to have a better technique of mass destruction than extermination camps and gas-ovens. Lock apparently held forth in this vein for several evenings; I was not there to hear him. Finally he piped up in my presence. I told him that even if he were merely all talk, as Skip claimed in his extenuation, such talk was not tolerated by civilized people. He could get out. He got, and was seen at the Club no more.

I have no doubt that basically the boy was sick, but some sicknesses are too infectious and too dangerous to harbour in a club full of impressionable youngsters.

In youth-work one constantly comes up against this problem of individuals who arouse one's sympathy and whom one wishes to help, but who are so impossibly anti-social that one simply can't afford to keep them in a club or similar organization because of the disruptive effect that they have upon the other members.

Of course youth workers vary in their degrees of tolerance towards these problem individuals. One Leader will be found struggling valiantly with a problem member long after another would have washed his hands of the case. Lock had been given a good run for his money; many might think that we had put up with him for too long!

Skip's other problem helper, Slim, had some time previously joined the Army which, rather surprisingly, seemed to suit him. He wrote long letters to Skip and Mr N., detailing his progress.

The Management Committee expressed interest in the boy's apparent reform and early in December Mr N. offered to read us one of Slim's letters. Of course we said we would love to hear it. So Mr N. took out the letter, opened it, and rather smugly started to read it aloud. It began with an account of the training-course that the boy was engaged on and then continued,

"You were always telling me in the old days to think less about myself and my own troubles and more of other people to get the chip off my shoulder. Well, I have been doing just that. Me and my mate, since the cold weather started, have been taking care of an old lady."

Here Mr N. glanced up at us all and smiled happily. Old Club bad-boy making good with a vengeance! We smiled back, delighted. Mr N. continued to read.

"We keep her in coal so she is never cold. We fetch the coal from a railway-siding near here; there is a big pile of the stuff and twice a week we go in a truck and lift enough of it to keep her in fires till we can get and fetch another load. She is ever so grateful. I thought you would like to know this."

Mr N's voice faltered. He looked up from his letter again. We all avoided his eyes.

Then, almost simultaneously, everyone burst out laughing. Only poor Mr N. remained mirthless.

He told me later that he had not read the letter right the way through himself before reading it to us. "I just glanced at it over my tea, noted that the boy said he had been helping somebody and decided to read it to the Committee to show that there was some good in the lad after all."

We now had fifty boys on our books and twenty-two girls. It was a "young club", sixty per cent of the members were still at school, which meant in effect, that fifty per cent of them were under sixteen. Yet the coterie of members actually making use of Club facilities for P.T., weight-training, music, discussion and so forth could not have numbered more than twenty.

The Youth Service people had been worrying about us for some time. The Club situation was certainly not a satisfactory one; a chaotic fringe-membership, as it were, of under-sixteens seething riotously but aimlessly, while a small, very exclusive In-Group of older members monopolized both the Club equipment and the time and attention of the Leader.

The Management Committee had by this time openly lost confidence in Skip. He, for his part, complained of lack of support and understanding from the Management Committee. All he got, he said, was criticism and interference.

It was true that the Management Committee had no understanding of Skip's methods or of his approach to youth-club work. We didn't understand what he was aiming at and his *laissez-faire* system bore no discernibly satisfactory results; indeed, quite the reverse. As the Youth Officer sagely observed of the friction between the Leader and the Management Committee, there were faults on both sides.

Finally Skip asked for a transfer. The Management Committee accepted his suggestion and applied for a new full-time Leader.

Skip left us early in December, his last appearance being at our Christmas Fair. During his final weeks with us he hurled himself into preparation for this Fair. He was clearly determined not to leave us with a whimper, but with a bang; for this I, at all events, admired him. Stimulated by his example of enthusiasm for the Fair the little boys, among them Midge and Gavin, built a space-ship sideshow for the kiddies, as they nicely put it (being so antique themselves) and after many evenings of sawing and painting they produced a six-foot high space-rocket apparently ready for blast-off, and effigies of Yogi Bear, Huckleberry Hound, and other popular T.V. personalities.

Upon the day of the Fair the rocket, Yogi Bear, Hound and all were arranged tableau-wise in a curtained recess and for threepence small children were able to file in, gaze their fill, then exit after pulling a wrapped gift from out of a bran-tub.

One saw, suddenly, in those last few weeks of the Skip era how much young people can achieve if they are given the right leadership. While it is perfectly true that they must not be coerced, they do need to be guided, stimulated, encouraged and sometimes cajoled. The right handling produces magical results.

Some alchemy now occurred between Skip and our members and they, who previously would not show the least co-operation over anything, threw themselves without stint into the business of the Christmas Fair.

When at last the day came we found ourselves with a toy stall, a handicraft stall, a paper-back book stall and a gift stall, as well as several sideshows. Most of the things on the stalls had been made by the members. There was nothing very splendid, but upon the other hand there was nothing trashy either. The Club was decorated throughout with home-made paper-chains and festoons. Besides the stalls and side-shows we had a raffle, a display of photographs, wall-newspapers and Club scrap-book and a film-show.

4

The film-show possessed the elements of farce and was quite the best part of the afternoon. It was made up of short films depicting various Club activities; the week-end adventurers apparently all asleep on the seats of a country railway-station; the Southend walkers dressed up like a troop of buskers; the Herne Bay week-end with everyone seemingly trying to hide behind a breakwater from aerial attack; and lastly the foot-ballers in their by now famous foul sequences of *ciné-verité*. The picture itself was minute, scarcely larger than a postage-stamp, but to compensate Skip had made a most ingenious sound-track on a tape-recorder and this was so stridently loud it almost raised one out of one's seat. The film-show was so successful that three or four performances were given and so Skip was kept hard at work on that, his last afternoon at the Club.

Real effort and enthusiasm had gone into this Fair, but alas, it was very poorly attended, partly because our Club was in an out-of-the-way part of the town and partly because few of our Club members had the kind of parents who were willing to support an enterprise of that nature.

Our only really encouraging moment was when the Mayor looked in. She chatted animatedly with the members, made generous purchases of things she could not possibly really have wanted, admired the space-rocket and Yogi Bear, and even wore her chain, as Midge remarked appreciatively.

But one mayor does not spell success, any more than one swallow makes a summer. The Treasurer, who was on the door, reported at the close of the afternoon that only fifty people had paid for admission (price threepence). Only ten small children had paid an extra threepence to see the rocket and Yogi Bear.

The total profits of the Fair amounted to ten pounds, five shillings and ninepence.

Oddly, all the raffle prizes were won by Club members. Since our Treasurer picked out the raffle-tickets at random from a large biscuit-tin it was virtually impossible to see how there could have been any fiddling. Yet Dolly won first-prize, Red the second, Sam the third, and Midge fourth prize. Most peculiar.

While the Treasurer, assisted by Fred, counted and then recounted the takings, Skip packed his final belongings, said good-bye to the members (they had bade him an official fare-well with a presentation the previous evening), shook hands with me (the rest of the Management Committee kept carefully out of the way), mounted his scooter and drove into the murk of an early December evening.

He made a great success of the Leadership of his next club.

Back in the hall after watching Skip drive away I found Midge and Gavin fastening brown paper round Yogi Bear and Huckleberry Hound. They explained to me that Skip had told them that they might have these to keep. They added, shyly, that they wanted me to have the space-rocket as a Christmas present.

I cannot think of any present that ever gave me more genuine pleasure, or proved more impossible, physically, to take to my bosom, than that six-foot high hard-board space-rocket.

I showed it to Mr N. and the Treasurer just before we locked up. "Look what I have been given as a Christmas present by two of the members."

"Very generous of 'em," said the Treasurer, "seeing that we paid for the materials they made it from and the tools they made it with."

"I know all that," I said, "but nevertheless it still means a lot."

"It means, my dear Mary," said the Treasurer, "that the little blighters haven't a clue what to do with it themselves and, knowing that you are a sucker for old junk and young gutter-snipes both, they have decided to pass the problem of rocket-disposal on to you."

"What are you going to do with it?" asked Mr N.

"God knows. I shall have to leave it down here for the time being until I've worked out some way of transporting it home."

"It'll look most ornamental, standing in your lounge," murmured the Treasurer.

"Come on, let's lock up; I've had enough of this place for one day," said Mr N. "Perhaps you'll turn out the lights in the canteen, while I see to the ones in the hall." He started walking towards the hall. I went to the canteen. Then he called, rather abruptly, "Madam Chairman."

"Yes," I called back.

"Has it occurred to you that we are on a seven p.m. to seven a.m. electricity tariff, yet the lights have been on since three-thirty p.m.?"

"Great Scot!" said the Treasurer. "So they have."

"But how could that be?" I said.

Mr N., who understood such matters, climbed on a chair and examined the time-switch. Then he climbed down off the chair.

"Has the switch been tampered with?" asked the Treasurer, anxiously.

"Let's put it this way," said Mr N., "it is certainly most odd that on the one afternoon when electric-light was essential, we have had a supply of off-tariff juice."

"But whoever would have done such a thing!" said the Treasurer, aghast.

"I have no idea," said Mr N., "but whoever it was should have, in my opinion, our heartfelt thanks. We should have looked a bunch of proper Charlies, trying to show the Mayor round a Christmas Fair in the dark."

"I never thought of that," I said.

"Nor I," said the Treasurer. "Completely escaped my mind, when we were making all the arrangements, that we'd have no lights because of that miserable tariff."

"I'll phone the Board first thing tomorrow and ask them to send someone round to adjust the clock and repair the seal," said Mr N. "Meantime let's be grateful that something, ahum, went wrong with the works, shall we?"

"Another prize example of what poor Mrs Z. means when she says that we do anti-social work," said the Treasurer. "Here we are, running a charity-bazaar with one hand and bilking the Electricity Board with the other."

Hot on the heels of the Christmas Fair we had a burglary. It was a ham-fisted affair, clearly the work of a juvenile, or juveniles. Access was gained through a window, the catch of which had been broken. Nineteen shillings were stolen from the petty-cash box in the office and a further fifteen shillings from Hal's Disc Fund. An animated attempt had been made to break open our antiquated safe (incidentally empty) but this had failed. Our villain, or villains, worn out by the struggle with the safe, had then refreshed himself, or themselves, with pop and chocolate from the canteen.

C.I.D. men came and searched for fingerprints. The fingerprints of Management Committee members, staff and sundry Club members were, of course, everywhere, but naturally of no assistance to the police, although it was strongly suspected that the miscreant, or miscreants, belonged to the Club. Indeed, later I was told the names of the guilty parties who were, sure enough, Club members.

Youth-clubs are, of course, always being broken into. It was surprising that we had never been burgled before; probably the fact that it was common knowledge that we were completely impoverished, with little on the premises worth stealing, alone had saved us from molestation. But now we had had a jumble-sale and a Christmas Fair in quick succession and it was reasonable to assume that there might be at least a few pounds in the office. Luckily such was not the case; I myself had arranged for all the cash to be taken home each night by a responsible person. In fact it was only due to a most unfortunate oversight that even the nineteen-shillings had been in the petty cash-box. The fifteen shillings of the Disc Fund had been Hal's responsibility; he had been warned not to leave any money on the premises and had replied loftily that he had faith in human nature.

Now he sat in the Leader's office cursing the filthy bastard who had walked off with the dosh. "Just wait till me and my mates lay hold of the bleeder. Stealing from kids. How low can you get?"

It emerged from his remarks that to steal the Disc Fund money was wholly reprehensible, since the money had been collected by the members themselves, but to steal nineteen shillings from Club petty-cash was not so bad since that had been, in some mysterious way, official or "government" money and therefore less sacrosanct.

The Club financial position was better now than it had ever been: we had over a hundred pounds in the bank, although of this seventy-five pounds was earmarked for the purchase of equipment. With the financial position thus eased I suggested that the Management Committee should throw a sherry-party for all the adults who had helped us: the Mayor, the canteen-ladies, members of local circles and associations, all those who had given us friendship during our recent months of struggle.

Objections were raised by one or two Management Committee members on the grounds that the young people would see adults drinking on the Club premises. My reply to that was

that we adults not infrequently saw some of the said young
people lurching into the Club in an advanced state of intoxica-
tion. The sight of a group of adults sipping sherry like civilized
beings would, I urged, be an educational one.

Even professional youth-workers disagree over the pros and
cons of this problem. Young people drink and get drunk, many
of their parents drink and get drunk; large numbers of teen-
agers are firmly of the opinion that alcohol is something you
take specifically in order to get drunk. They know nothing of
the more sophisticated virtues of drink. Some youth-leaders
believe that it is right to teach young people to develop a
civilized adult attitude towards drinking, while others believe
that alcohol should remain firmly beyond the pale of every
youth organization.

Management Committee discussion of the proposed sherry
party was prolonged, but perfectly amicable in spite of diver-
gence of opinion. Finally one or two people said that although
they wished the party well they would prefer to be excused
from attending, while most of the others seemed to feel that the
thing would be all right so long as it took place early in the
evening before the Club opened so that the Club members need
not be exposed to the hazards of seeing adults drinking sherry
on the Club premises.

Invitations were planned for six o'clock in the evening and it
was decided to postpone the Club opening for half-an-hour;
thereby giving us an hour-and-a-half for the party.

The Treasurer asked about the electric-light: how did we
propose to illuminate the party? It then transpired that
although a man from the Electricity Board had been down to
the Club to see about our tariff-supply and to correct the clock
and repair the seal, for some inexplicable reason we were still
able to get juice all round the twenty-four hours.

This led to some very perplexed discussion indeed.

"We are bilking the Board, Madam Chairman," declared
Mrs Z., repeatedly.

"No we aren't," said Mr N. "We were bilking the Board at
the Christmas Fair (excuse me, through the Chair), but we had
the electricity people down here immediately afterwards to put
the matter right. We were completely open with them. If they
can't repair the time switch so that it works that isn't our
responsibility."

"Exactly," said the Vice-Chairman. "Up to the Board to see that their tariff-system works."

"That may be so, but nevertheless strictly speaking, Madam Chairman, we are bilking the Board," said Mrs Z.

"Not at all, Madam Chairman," said the Treasurer. "The tom-fool Board are bilking themselves."

"Hear hear," said Mr N.

"May I propose, Madam Chairman," said the Secretary, "that we leave the Board to make the next move. We've informed them that we are receiving off-tariff electricity and asked them to put the matter right. That they have failed to do so isn't our responsibility. It's up to them to get us back on our tariff. We've notified them; we've discharged our duty as law-abiding citizens. Leave them to make the next move to get things right; at all events until after the sherry-party."

"I second that," said the Vice-Chairman.

The proposal was then put to the vote and duly carried.

After this plans for the party went smoothly ahead. Sherry, soft-drinks and cocktail-nibbles of a conservative description were ordered and glasses hired. The Club lounge was made as clean and attractive as a lounge can be made when it has gravy-brown second-hand lino, spavined second-hand chairs and a leak in the roof. We invited over twenty people and all but one accepted the invitation.

During the afternoon of the day of the party a pea-souper of Dickensian quality, ochrous and dense, such as we had not seen for many a year, blanketed our town and the surrounding area. I had been planning to wear an elegant little cocktail number but finally groped my way forth in fur-lined boots and tweeds. Traffic had come to a standstill. The fog was icy-cold and smelt like the knife-powder which had been used in the scullery in my infancy and which I had quite forgotten until I smelt this fog. Thinking of knife-powder and feeling like Mrs Todgers I fumbled my way for an interminable mile or so from my door to the door of the Club.

Outside the Club stood the Vice-Chairman with a large suit-case containing the drinks. He was hopping first on one leg and then on the other and clapping his hands to keep warm. He said, "Good-evening. Jinxed again."

"You're telling me. Isn't it ghastly? Has Sophie arrived yet with the keys?"

Sophie was our cleaner and caretaker.

"I haven't seen a soul. I've been here twenty minutes," said the Vice-Chairman.

"Don't say she's not turning up."

"I doubt if anyone will turn up on a night like this."

We stood waiting outside the Club for another ten minutes, then it was decided that I should collect the keys from Sophie, who fortunately lived in the next street. I reached her house after cannily feeling my way along several fences and a privet-hedge; she was in her front-room watching television. She had in fact been invited to the party, the arrangement having been that she should arrive a little before time, with the keys: now she explained that she wasn't coming to the party as her husband had 'flu.

I put the keys in my handbag and tried returning to the Club. I lost myself completely. I was on the point of becoming desperate, even a little panicky, when I heard a bicycle-bell ring far too close to me for safety and Midge's well-known voice shouting something indistinct about "a nice old night for a carve-up." I shouted in my turn, loudly, "Midge!" Then Gavin bellowed, "Hey, that's Mrs B.!"

"Gavin. Oi!" I shouted again.

"Blimey, Mrs B., I was pretty well right on top of you," said Midge, still invisible. I could hear him dismounting from a bike which now scrunched to a standstill a few feet from me. "What you standing hollering here in the middle of the road for?"

"I'm lost."

"Lost? Where you trying to go?" Midge now emerged from the fog, holding his bike.

"To the Club of course."

"Cor mate, listen to this. It's ripe." Midge turned to an invisible Gavin. "Here's old Mrs B. bleedin' well lost herself five feet away from the flipping doorstep!"

Gavin began laughing; Midge laughed too. The Vice-Chairman's voice came muffled from the fog. "Is that Mrs B. there?"

"Yeah, we got her, guv," shouted Midge. He and Gavin then steered me to the Club. I was only a few yards from it. The Vice-Chairman said, "Much more waiting about like this and I shall start helping myself to sherry from sheer self-preservation."

"Great idea. Let's get inside and open a bottle," I said. "Anyone else arrived yet?"

"Not a soul."

I unlocked the door and the Vice-Chairman and I entered the Club. We told Midge and Gavin that they couldn't come in until seven-thirty. Although they, and all the other members, were supposed to know of this all ready, they both made a great display of indignation. "Cor, stone-it. I like that. 'Ere's you lot gonna be in the warm having a nosh-up while us lot's left outside in the bleedin' fog!"

"Mind your language, you two lads," said the Vice-Chairman. He added to me, "Warm, they call it. The place is like an ice-box."

Gradually a few other Management Committee members appeared, together with two canteen-ladies and then the Mayor and Mayoress. We huddled in the lounge, all with our coats on, sipping sherry and being bravely cheerful. Presently my husband arrived. He said, "Why are all those wretched little kids shut outside there on the pavement?"

"Kids outside? They shouldn't be turning up here tonight until seven-thirty."

"Well there they are. Can't you hear them?"

We paused to listen. A small, but vociferous mob could be heard stamping on the pavement, kicking the door, hollering and shouting.

"They can't come in until our party's over."

"Don't be ridiculous, Mary. You can't leave the poor little blighters out there on a night like this. They'll freeze to death."

"Oh do please let them in!" exclaimed the Mayor. The Mayoress and the canteen-ladies echoed the request and my husband marched off towards the front-door. I pattered after him in agitation.

"Look, I was only allowed to hold this sherry-party on the distinct understanding that none of the Club members would be present during the actual . . . "

"I refuse to aid and abet an act of cruelty to children," he said.

He opened the front-door and at once a host of boys stampeded into the Club bellowing, "Wheresa booze?"

They charged into the lounge and seized cocktail-biscuits, gherkins, pretzels and the rest from under the noses of our

4*

guests. To do the Mayor and Mayoress justice they sat in the midst of the seething mass of scuffling, gobbling, shouting juveniles and laughed. I stood helplessly by and intoned to the Vice-Chairman, who was similarly dumb-founded by this turn of events,

" 'The Assyrian came down like a wolf on the fold . . . ' ".

"Very apt indeed," he said.

Fortunately the members made no attempt to drink the sherry, which they said they didn't like, but contented themselves with all the food and the soft-drinks, which they gulped down with staggering rapidity, meantime wisecracking and joking in the most buoyant manner.

Afterwards we apologized to the Mayor and Mayoress for the startling style in which the party had disintegrated, rather than ended, but they replied that they had enjoyed every minute of the evening. They felt, they said, that they really had been to a youth-club.

The final bizarre touch was that when we all stepped out of the Club into the street at seven-thirty the fog had quite lifted. It had apparently fallen from the sky like a giant pall specifically to prevent our guests reaching the Club and, having spoiled the party, had dispersed as if by a few magic puffs from a Djin.

PART THREE

UNCLUBABLES SQUARED

" . . . adults might well strengthen their links with young people."

Youth Service. Vol. 4. 2/February 1964.
(M.O.E. publication)

CHAPTER X

PUTTING ON THE GLOVES

TWELVE MONTHS OF *laissez-faire* policy had indeed left our Club a rowdy, undisciplined, aggressive place. Fights broke out amongst the members at the slightest provocation. There was a decided tendency towards vandalism. Doors were kicked in and windows broken. Furniture was mutilated.

We had been warned that it might be some considerable time before a new full-time Leader could be found; the situation was even worse than it had been two years previously. Of our two assistant Leaders Bonny C. slipped a disc and was right out of action, while Timothy W. was also forced by ill-health to be absent a lot. Management Committee members put in all the time they could at the Club, but even so it was exceedingly difficult to keep the place going.

Our paid-up members consisted of thirty-three boys and eighteen girls. The majority of the boys were over seventeen; most of the younger ones, including Midge and Gavin, had now ceased to come to the Club. There is always a strong degree of animosity between senior and junior boys in a club and, unless the Leader is vigilant, the older boys will do their best to oust the younger ones. With Skip gone and no professional full-time staff present to keep a close and constant eye on things, our younger boys had been excluded by their elders.

The majority of our girls, on the other hand, continued to be, as they had been for some months past, on the young side. Of our eighteen girls only five were over fifteen. These few older girls were steady, intelligent, charming; they had little influence however over the younger girls, who formed a tight and rather tarty society of their own. Their ringleaders were Dee and Dolly.

These two girls, each within a mere few weeks of becoming fifteen, were increasingly unclubable. Dee's language was so hair-raising that even our Vice-President, an old professional soldier, declared that it shook him. Since Dee's obscenities were not part of her natural, everyday speech, but were used with the intent to insult or to shock, I came down upon them as strongly as anyone.

As Dee's vocabulary became bluer and bluer so did Dolly's eye-paint. She experimented, too, with iridescent streaks of sea-green and sepia under-eye liner, spreading the colours virtually across the upper half of her face. Meantime her hair rose higher and higher, more and more stiffly lacquered. Dolly spoke rarely, but tittered a lot, her titters showing an increasing tendency to turn into short, high-pitched yelps. Whenever she yelped I looked and almost always when I looked there would be a boy moving away from her with a pleased smile on his face. Often the boy in question would be Chuck.

Cockney in extraction, short, stocky yet physically powerful, Chuck was sexually very attractive. I don't think he was really more seriously inclined towards Dolly than he was to any of the other girls, but she certainly inclined towards him. The mere sight of him was enough to make her gasp and yip.

Finally, as the result of a series of exceptionally high-pitched yelps from Dolly, together with assurances that she was black-and-blue all over from him, I suggested to Chuck that perhaps he should leave her alone. He looked aggrieved. "Stone it, Mrs B., use your eyes. Who's pesterin' who?"

It was interesting to learn, from a source outside the Club, that Dolly spent week-end evenings baby-sitting and that she was a very good baby-sitter indeed. "Really reliable, and a wonderful way with them."

One day I discovered her, in a neighbouring street, stooping over a pram gazing with adoring eyes at a particularly robust baby whose great cheeks bloomed like peonies. I stopped to speak to Dolly and commented on the baby. Dolly looked up at me, smiling. "Ain't he smashing? I'm minding him."

"You like babies?"

The smile broadened. "Yeah. Smashing."

"Have you any brothers or sisters?"

"Yeah. Seven of us. I'm the oldest."

"So you get plenty of baby-minding at home, too?"

"Yeah. They're a smashing lot."

Further conversation revealed that she always helped her mum put the little ones to bed at night before she came down to the Club.

This was an interesting sidelight on Dolly's true personality and went far, I felt, to counterbalance the eye-paint and the titters. In fact Dolly's trouble was that she was so horribly dumb. Her great, round eyes stared out, bovine and trusting, from under her parakeet-hued lids, she wielded her green and violet eyeshadow-sticks with grubby, childish hands. She was indeed a sheep in wolf's clothing. Unfortunately the young wolves who prowled around her were all genuine.

Since Skip's departure we had reverted to being a really tough club. Thicks and roughs once more began to bomb up on their motor-bikes. Clem and several of his mates abandoned the rival club round the corner and joined us again; but Cleopatra, Rosebud and Howard didn't return. They had outgrown youth-clubs altogether.

There was no doubt that Chuck was now emerging as our Club's most outstanding personality. He was amazingly versatile; he could lift impressive weights, dive from dizzy heights, swim further than he could walk, quell a riot, tactfully handle a Cube, run up curtains on the sewing-machine, chair a meeting, referee a fight, brew an excellent cup of tea, was handy with hammer and nails, and could sing very pleasingly when sufficiently tight. We adults found ourselves relying upon him increasingly. Some sort of an anchor-man is essential to a youth-club. Chuck was born for the role. He could be trusted with any problem.

His attitude towards me as Chairman of the Management Committee was courteous, at times distinctly paternal. None the less he made it gently clear that he took me with a pinch of salt.

Not only did we adults find that Chuck was a natural leader; the other members also distinctly saw him in the same light. Fortunately he had considerable influence over the toughs; largely because he could knock any of them flat any time he wished. This was comforting, because things could get somewhat dicey down at the Club these days.

One murky February evening I arrived at the Club a few minutes after seven to do an evening's duty with Timothy W. and Mrs Z. I found Mrs Z. alone; she had opened the Club and was now starting up the canteen. She said,

"Thank goodness you've come. I was in fear and trembling that I'd be landed here on my jack. Tim hasn't arrived yet and there are some real ripe beauties trickling in tonight, I can tell you. Funny how you don't see them for weeks on end, and then they all turn up together, isn't it?"

By ripe beauties she meant our real young villains. I glanced round with as casual an air as I could manage. One or two of the boys certainly were the sort to make one uneasy. I said, "Well, let's hope Tim turns up before things really start humming."

We got the canteen under way; kettles boiling, milk, coffee, sugar set out, hot-dogs heating and so forth. Mrs Z. said, "If you've anything to see to in the office I can cope here."

I went into the Leader's office and started opening the Club mail. While we were without a Leader I was doing all the paper-work; there was a staggering amount.

I opened a brochure about a week-end climbing course in North Wales. As I sat reading it two of our particularly villainous eighteen-year-olds came slouching in, leather-clad and lowering. "Can you 'an us the darts?"

I handed them the darts, which were kept in a drawer of the Leader's desk. "Don't you want the board too?"

"No, lady. Gonna chuck darts at each other. New game. Lose an eye and the other bloke scores a bull."

"I wouldn't put you past it." I handed them the dart-board.

"We're a tough lot down here," said the larger of the two; a boy with a nasty reputation as a street-fight bully.

"So I've heard."

"Yeah, we're tough, us lot."

"So I hear."

"Yeah, I'm telling you, we're tough!" Suddenly he became bad-tempered and aggressive, thrusting his face towards me. It was unpleasant. However to quail was to be defeated from the word go. So I patted him kindly on his leather-clad shoulder (with a show of nerve I inwardly didn't possess) and said, "No, no, you're not tough yet, but you will be by the time I've finished with you."

The sheer effrontery of this literally took his breath away. When he had got it back he said, "Wotcha mean?"

"You're not tough yet, you lot, but in the end maybe you'll make the grade."

"What you gonna do to make us lot tough, hey?" Now he was amused.

"Well, for a start, can you do that?" I showed him the climbing-course brochure with its picture of a boy rappelling off a rock-face. My friend glared at it.

"Me do that? Them flippin' Dook's rope-tricks? Not bleeding likely. Got more sense."

"You couldn't do it," I said.

"Don't want to, mate."

"I'm disappointed in you both," I said.

"Wheresa sense innit?"

"Some people enjoy it," I said.

"Orright then, let 'em. Only don't expect us to do it."

"What about some Italian sunshine then, instead? That more your mark?" I handed them another brochure, this one about a ten-day trip to Verona for youth-club parties. They stared at it. "Wheresat?"

"Verona."

"Wot the hell's Vrona?"

"Italian town. Where Romeo and Juliet came from."

"Gergh. They wasn't real."

"They were, though."

"Wotcha do there?" asked one boy. The other said, grinning broadly, "Same as old Romeo an' Juliet done, tosh."

"How muchit cost?"

"Says on the back of that paper you're holding," I said.

"You don't need to go alla way to Italy for that," remarked the broadly grinning boy. His mate said,

"Sunny Italy, mate. Lie in the nood on a nice hot beach. Wouldn't mind it."

"What, lie in the nood with a youth-club party? Blimey, you're hopeful. Don't think there'd be much chance o' that."

Laughing and joking they withdrew with the board and darts. I heaved a long sigh of relief. That at least was the back of them for a bit.

The telephone rang. It was Tim's wife to say that he was in bed with quinsies.

I went to the canteen to tell Mrs Z. this unwelcome news. She said, "It never rains but it pours."

Dolly was seated on a bar-stool. She smiled and offered me a wine-gum. I accepted it and said, conversationally, "You'll be sorry to hear that poor Tim W. has quinsies."

Dolly's eyes brightened, a sentimental leer broke over her face. "Oo-oo! Littel gels or littel boys?"

Back in the office I kept the door open and every now and again popped out to see what was happening in the rest of the building. Chuck was superintending a session with the vaulting-horse, while another group of boys played handball. A knot of

well-known troublemakers, including the two who had just
been talking to me in the office, were lounging and larking by
the darts-board. There was something about them which
instinctively made me apprehensive; from them tension
radiated tonight. I noticed Mrs Z. furtively watching them
through the canteen-hatch; she caught my eye and we
exchanged fleeting, unhappy grimaces.

In the lounge two or three couples were seated, mildly
snogging. Two of these couples were, I knew, unofficially
engaged. Snogging is not to be encouraged in youth-clubs, but
at what point does light-hearted patting and pawing each
other around (much in the way puppies play) become actual
snoggery? Especially when between the unofficially engaged? I
was pondering the niceties of this when I heard sounds of real
hubbub coming from the big hall. Stamping, banging, shouting,
whistling; a fight was on.

Before I had decided what was my best course of action Hal
charged in. "Can I have the gloves, Mrs B.? They want 'em
for a fight." He began rummaging in the sports gear cupboard
for the boxing-gloves.

"See, what Chuck does these days when there'sa fight is make
'em put the gloves on and fight proper, steada carving and
kicking one another an' all that jazz. Best way, innit?"

"I suppose so. But look here Hal, we don't want any
trouble . . . "

Hal found the gloves, grabbed hold of me and said, "Won't
be no trouble. Old Chuck knows what he's doing. Come on. You
gotta be the judge."

"Judge!" I said in horror. I found myself being hustled into
the hall. "Yeah, old Chuck's Ref. You gotta be judge. Must've
a judge. Must do it proper."

At that time we had in the hall five upright pianos. One, the
only one in decent condition, was the official club piano. Of the
other four one was a survivor of the jumble-sale and the other
three had been given us by the sort of people who give youth-
clubs moribund upright pianos. Of no possible use to us, we had
to date been unable to think of how to get rid of them. Bar of
course passing them on to a fellow youth-club; that was
against our principles.

These pianos had now been arranged to define an impro-
vised boxing-ring. Twenty-five or so youths, in the seventeen to

twenty-one age-bracket, crowded round this ring area, shouting, shoving, whistling and stamping. I could not see beyond
their black leather backs.

"Here'sa gloves, an' the judge!" bellowed Hal. He tossed
the gloves over the heads of the milling onlookers. Two of the
footballers seized me, lifted me up and sat me on top of a piano.

I now had a good view over the heads of the rest of the
audience. The stage floodlights had been switched on to
illuminate the scene of action. Chuck, looking perfectly cool,
was already tying the gloves on one boy, whom I at once
recognized as my tough conversationalist of earlier that
evening. He was keeping up a non-stop flow of insults and
obscenities directed towards his opponent, a much quieter,
thinner, red-haired boy of about the same age; Pete (I didn't
know his other name). Hal now stepped forward and put the
gloves on Pete, who was standing pale and utterly silent. It
seemed to me that neither boy was eager for a formal fight, despite
the grim pallor of the one and the non-stop insults of the other.

I probably felt more frightened than either of them, had the
truth been known. It was clear that it needed only the merest
spark to set off a general free-for-all; one of those terrifying all-
in club fights. I was numbly envisaging this possibility when
Chuck glanced in my direction and sang out, "O.K., Mrs B.?"

"Chuck, I don't want any trouble, understand?" I shouted.
He raised his hand in a species of buoyant salute and shouted
back, "There won't be no trouble, duck."

He and Hal then roared for general silence. Chuck
announced in truly professional sing-song style that it would be
a six-round contest of one minute rounds and recited the
customary warning about a clean fight and so forth. The dark
boy fidgeted and muttered. Chuck told them to start boxing
and stepped neatly aside as the opponents, neither of whom
knew how to box, though each had a name for street-fighting,
started to belt one another in a furious, but unscientific, manner.

The audience meantime cheered, whistled, jeered and placed
bets. At the end of the first round the assailants were forcibly
pulled apart by Chuck and Hal, who also acted as seconds.
Chuck instructed both boys to relax and breathe deeply; Pete
stood inhaling and exhaling concentratedly, but the other boy
now became involved in a swearing, heaving struggle with Hal.
Hal grabbed at him; the boy broke away from Hal, at the same

time dealing him a hefty kick on the shin. Hal yelled and kicked back, just as Chuck gave a signal for the next round to begin. The two opponents thereupon rushed at one another with a fresh jumble of blows; the dark boy had his mouth open cursing non-stop and it was clear that he was going to run out of breath first. Both boys looked grimly desperate and the audience, during this second round, became quite silent. Then Pete tripped and at the same time swung out his right fist and caught his blaspheming enemy a hard smack on the nose. There was a dramatic gush of blood, the boy who had been struck staggered, Chuck stopped the fight and forced the antagonists, before they knew where they were, to shake hands. The bleeding loser refused, in the middle of the ceremony, to go through with it and started cursing again like mad. Chuck said, "Shake hands proper, you berk, or I'll flatten you." The two boys then shook hands properly.

The defeated boy, who began snivelling, his nose bleeding most profusely, was led away by two pals. "He arst for it," said Fred.

"Funny . . . all that blood," said Pete, staring at his smeared gloves. Chuck started untying them for him.

I got down from the piano; my knees were shaking. "Thank you Chuck," I said. "You handled that very well. It could've been nasty."

"Always best to make 'em put the gloves on, duck," said Chuck. "Better'n bicycle-chains."

Chuck, Hal, Pete and I then repaired to the canteen to have a coffee each on the house. But in the canteen we found poor Mrs Z. in tears, while our neighbour, Mrs X., was vehemently haranguing nobody in particular upon the evils of fighting. When she saw me she sprang at me, shouting, "Animals! That's what this lot are. Animals!"

"Good heavens, Mrs X., what on earth is the matter?" I said. She wasn't listening. "No better'n beasts, and what's more you . . . "

"I hate fights, I hate fights," sobbed Mrs Z. "You shouldn't let them fight, Mary."

"Uncivilized lot! Disgusting!" shrilled Mrs X.

"It was a perfectly good, clean fight," I said. "In fact it's one of the first signs of real civilization that I've seen down here."

Mrs X. squealed, "Fights are for animals!"

I sat down on a stool. "We want four coffees please," I said to

Mrs Z. She sobbed back, "Make them yourselves. I'm too upset."

Mrs X. continued to screech; "Teach 'em to sit down to a conf'rence table! Talk things out!"

"Nonsense," I said. "There's nothing wrong with a simple, straight-forward fight on an occasion like this." Then, to Mrs Z., "Let's have those coffees, my dear. You have one too."

The infuriated Mrs X. seized my legs and tried to pull me from the stool. "Violence! That's all you Tory lot can think of!"

"I can't conceive, Mrs X., why you should leap to the conclusion that I am a . . . "

"Loada savages!"

I clung to the stool with my hands and held my legs rigid while she clawed at my ankles. I had a passionate longing to kick out at her with my feet, but restrained myself because icy calm on my part was obviously the tactic which would flurry her most. Meantime Chuck, Hal and Pete watched in astonishment mingled with keen enjoyment. Mrs Z. had moved to the back of the canteen and was standing there wiping her eyes with her handkerchief and trying to control herself; she didn't see what was happening. Mrs X. yelped convulsively, "Loada savages!"

I hung grimly to the stool (otherwise I should have found myself on the floor) and said, as blandly as I could, "Precisely why are you here, Mrs X? Did you wish to have a chat with me about something?"

"I come in here first place on account of the dreadful noise . . ."

"You had no right to come in. You should have remained outside on the step and asked if you might speak either to Mrs Z. or myself."

"Stopped on the step! Ask if I might . . . ! Who the bleeding hell d'you think you are?" She dropped my feet in her indignation.

"I'm the Chairman of this Club and I must ask you to leave. You are trespassing."

"My stars, I never heard anything like it!"

I turned round to the fascinated boys. "Chuck."

"Yes, Mrs B.?"

"Perhaps you would be kind enough to escort this lady to the door."

"Pleasure," said Chuck.

Mrs X. gave me a look of total hatred and was then walked out very quickly by Chuck, with Hal marching a step or two behind.

Mrs Z., mixing instant-coffee in a tea-cup, now advanced upon me in her turn. "You should have stopped them fighting, Mary. We aren't here to encourage fights. It is our duty to teach them better."

"You can just see me stopping that lot," I said, bitterly.

"I hate fights. They must be taught not to fight. They're dreadful things, dreadful."

"For heaven's sake give it a rest, I'm on the verge of collapse," I said. "Let's have that coffee and forget it."

Chuck and Hal now returned from escorting Mrs X. to the door. They were both grinning broadly.

"Cheer up, Mrs B.," said Hal. "That old bag won't be bothering us again in a hurry."

"Fixed her orright," said Chuck.

"Whatever d'you do to her?" gasped Mrs Z.

"Nothing, nothing," said Chuck, lightly. He produced a packet of cigarettes. "Just told her a thing or two what's healthy for her to know." He offered me a cigarette. "Talked to her straight." His grin grew broader. He offered Mrs Z. a cigarette; she declined it with a weak wave of the hand.

She served us coffees. Pete gave me a blow-by-blow account of his end of the fight.

"I didn't think I stood a chance. I was that outa breath. My legs felt all wonky, too. See, I never worn gloves before. They're heavy. I thought, I shall never knock this geezer down in a montha Sundays. I just hit out, hit anything an' kept hitting and alla sudden I found I'd landed him a beauty. And all that blood. He went off blubbering, d'you know?"

"He got what was coming to him, mate," said Hal. "Mark my words, it'll do him a world of good."

"That geezer's bin askin' for a good knockin' down for a long time," said Chuck.

I was thankful when the Club closed and I could go home. I felt worn out.

Mrs Z. gave me a lift to the bus-station. She said, "And just to think that we do this voluntarily. Just to think we could spend our evenings doing floral decoration."

The Management Committee had decided that before a new full-time Leader arrived the Club must be thoroughly spring-cleaned, redecorated and put into first-rate order. A full inventory of equipment must be made, too. The Vice-Chairman and I undertook to do the inventory. We commenced upon a grand turning-out of drawers, boxes and cupboards.

Over the months masses of rubbish had accumulated. For several successive evenings my companion and I sorted through the stuff, dumping in the lounge all the junk we found. The members were allowed to salvage anything they fancied from this pile of junk; everything that they left went into the dustbins.

Both the Vice-Chairman and I picked up fleas. We stood scratching ourselves and coughing from the clouds of dust. "I s'pose you could call this youth-work," said he, "but I feel more like a rag-and-bone man myself than one of that dedicated band of men and women whom the nation cannot ever thank enough."

There was still an awful lot of petting going on amongst the Club members. The Vice-Chairman and I agreed that it would have to stop. We informed the couples concerned of this firm decision; they replied that they were all unofficially engaged. "Surely it's orright for a bird to sit on her chap's knee, Mrs B., when they're unofficially engaged?" I said that engagements, unofficial or official, made no difference to the rule of petting on the Club premises. The kids replied that I was a blooming square. The Vice-Chairman added his voice to mine: he too was told that he was a square. "Just because you're too darn old for a bit of a snog," said Petunia, who was sitting comfortably on Mike's knee. The Vice-Chairman (in his early forties) leapt furiously at Petunia and hauled her to her feet, saying explosively that what the Club needed was discipline. Petunia shrieked and clung to Mike. There was a species of tug-of-war and then Petunia broke away and ran off crying. Mike jumped up, swearing at the Vice-Chairman, and then ran after the girl. The Vice-Chairman retired into the Leader's office and said something most unrestrained about Petunia. I pretended not to hear and resumed cleaning out a cupboard.

"It's certainly a very difficult problem when they're engaged," said Tim. "When they're not engaged it's different, plain sailing then; but all these older, engaged couples . . . "

"We seem suddenly to have an awful lot of engaged couples," I said. "The entire Club membership seems to be on the verge of getting spliced."

"I'll splice the bleeding lot of 'em in a way they don't expect if they continue behaving in this bolshie fashion," said the Vice-Chairman. "Why the hell should I stand for being answered back by a silly little chit of a kid no older than my own daughter?"

Later that evening I asked Dee, who was twisting absorbedly by herself to a Chubby Checker disc, what precisely was the difference between being unofficially and officially engaged. When did an unofficial engagement become official? Clearly it was not a matter of public announcement because everybody knew about the unofficial engagement. Dee, in between changing the Chubby Checker disc for Billy Fury, replied,

"Why, it's when your chap gives you the ring."

"And after you're officially engaged d'you go to bed with him?"

"Cor, Mrs B.!" said Lana, who was standing nearby, varnishing a coffee-table. Dee started giggling like mad. Lana said, "You don't do that till you're married."

"I'm only asking," I said. "I like to get my information authentic."

"If the bloke's gonna do that he'll do it as soon as you'll let him, ring or no ring, official or unofficial," said Dee. "Official's got nothing to do with that."

"Thank you, Dee," I said. "That's what I want to know."

"Ask away," said Dee. "Anything else?"

"D'you always get married, following an official engagement? I mean, obviously you can break-off an unofficial engagement, but how does a girl feel about breaking-off an official one?"

"Well," said Dee, "naturally you think twice before you give a fellow back his ring."

"You really take an official engagement seriously?"

"Yes, definitely."

"But an unofficial engagement not so seriously?"

"An unofficial engagement's when you're trying each other out, innit?" said Lana.

"What exactly d'you mean by trying each other out?"

"Why, getting to know each other. Going steady together, and all that."

"Yeah," said Dee. "Like finding out what his manners are in the back seat of the pictures."

"You ever been engaged, Dee?" I said.

"No," said Dee. "I've had a chap, though."

"Liar," said Lana.

Dee smiled enigmatically and turned on Billy Fury full-blast. Lana pulled a face to convey to me that Dee was showing-off and I wasn't to believe a word. I was not so sure.

The next evening found the Vice-Chairman and myself clearing out yet another cupboard. The record-player deafened us with the inevitable Chubby Checker and Billy Fury; Dee remained alone in a corner, twisting, twisting. Some of the other little girls twisted too, but they soon got bored with it. Not so Dee. On and on she twisted.

The Vice-Chairman and I threw out a great pile of old magazines. They gradually built up into a species of cairn in the corner of the lounge. Chuck began idly raking through them. Dolly, who was now twisting with Dee, broke off to join Chuck in turning over the magazines. Soon she gave one of her high-pitched yelps. She picked up a magazine called *How To Do It Yourself*, covered the word *Yourself* with her hand and held out the magazine for Chuck to see. "Look, Chuck. This magazine. *How To Do It*. We don't need ter read that, do we?" And off she went into a Niagara of titters.

Chuck gave a guffaw, then realized I was watching and turned away from Dolly and her magazine. She continued to titter.

I said to the Vice-Chairman, "For the first time in the history of this Club sex is really rearing its ugly head."

"Exactly what I mean," he said. "Once it starts it's like an epidemic." He knocked two mildewy cricket-pads together despondently. "We'll have to jump on it."

The rest of the evening we saw nothing to jump on. Dolly had a coke in the canteen, twisted a bit, had a coffee. Chuck retired to do some weight-lifting. Petunia, Lana and two new members, twins, Sally and Sue, played table-tennis. Mike, Hal, Clem and Fred played darts. Billy Fury moaned, Chubby Checker chanted.

Next evening I was once again clearing out rubbish. Presently I saw Chuck walk quickly up the big hall and disappear behind the pianos, which were now drawn up together in a sort of palisade. Then I saw Dolly trip blithely up the hall and go behind the pianos too. I heard her tittering, then yelp. Tim also heard the yelp and glanced towards the pianos. "What d'you suppose is going on there?" I said, putting down some old net-curtaining I was sorting. "Nothing much, Mrs B., they're all being very nice and quiet tonight," said Timothy. A sweet soul; genuinely innocent.

I waited a moment, then went up the hall towards the pianos. At that instant Dolly's much disarrayed head of hair appeared round a piano, with great bosky eyes peering. She noticed me and squealed. At once Chuck dived out, very friendly.

"What the hell's going on?" I said.

"Nothing duck," said Chuck. "Want me to help you sort the old boxing-gear? You said you would."

Dolly now emerged from behind the pianos, twitching her blouse into place. She gave me a sweet smile and scuttled away fast in the direction of the girls' powder-room.

I marched back to Tim. "Look, let's get rid of those pianos."

"There's nothing wrong with them. They only need to be tuned."

"Nevertheless get rid of them."

"We can't find anyone who wants them."

"Then chop them up. Have a bonfire."

"We can't do that! They were given us in good faith, for Club use."

"Use them as a Club gift of firewood for old-age pensioners."

Poor Tim was aghast. "But suppose the people who gave them to us find out that we've used them for firewood?"

"Suppose they find out what we're using them for now?"

Poor Tim was all at sea. He repeated, "They only need tuning."

The following two evenings I didn't go to the Club but on the third evening I did. I stepped into the office to find the Vice-Chairman waiting for me. He said, without preamble, "Mary we've got to get rid of those ruddy pianos."

"I've already asked Tim to get them chopped up," I said.

"Good. Then let's get 'em chopped up, pronto. The less natural cover we have in this place the better." He made sure the door was properly shut and then continued, "I was down here last night when I heard some very funny noises coming from behind those pianos. So I took off my shoes, ran very quick up the hall in my socks and looked over the top of the piano and there was that young Dolly and a boy. She was stripped to the waist. I said to her, 'Put your things on, get out of here and don't come back.' She put on her jumper and ran. I had a word with the boy. He won't do that again; not down here, anyway, I'll lay a bet."

The result was that all the pianos, bar one, were converted into firewood for pensioners. Dolly's father sent us a message that she would not be attending the Club in future as he had decided to keep her at home at nights.

We spotted no more incidents of the sort that the Vice-Chairman had interrupted but discipline in general continued to be poor, despite all our efforts. Several members were suspended for horse-play, drunkenness and vandalism. The period of suspension from the Club was a fortnight.

Mr N., Tim and I suspended people in the sense that they were debarred from the Club, but our Vice-Chairman suspended them literally. One night he noticed a boy sky-larking amongst the girls in a manner most unpleasant. The Vice-Chairman warned the boy. The boy ignored the warning. The Vice-Chairman said, "Look, I've warned you once. I'm not warning you again. Next time you do that you'll regret it."

"Why, what'll you do?" jeered the boy.

"You'll be suspended."

"That'll hurt."

"You'll be suspended, my friend. I shall hang you on those hooks," said the Vice-Chairman, indicating a set of hooks protruding, coat-peg style, from the lounge wall. The boy said, "Just you try it, guv."

The Vice-Chairman thereupon picked up the boy and hung him on the hooks in the manner in which one hangs up a wet coat to dry. The hooks caught in the boy's jacket and there the miscreant dangled, too astounded to utter a syllable or even to move, while the other members roared with laughter. After what seemed an appropriate period the Vice-Chairman unhooked the boy and set him on his feet. Without a word the boy left the Club. The Vice-Chairman more than half expected to meet with reprisals, but none came. The boy stayed away from the Club for a few nights, then returned. We had no more trouble from him. In fact, in course of time, he became very friendly.

Dee's fondness for bad language whipped up the other little girls into a frenzy of swearing and obscenities. One young thing became particularly bad, until at last the Vice-Chairman, without comment, handed her a beaker of water and a piece of soap floating in it. The girl said, "What's all this?"

"To rinse your mouth out with. I think you need it."

Again it worked. We did not hear nearly so much trooper-style language after that.

In the canteen I caught a boy stealing sugar. He had both

hands full of cubes of the stuff. I said, "And now what are you going to do with all that?"

"I asked for a cup of coffee, didn't I? Need sugar for my coffee, don't I?"

"You've got at least a pound of it there."

"Got a sweet tooth an' all."

"O.K.," I said, "so long as you are going to have it all in your coffee. I just don't want to see it wasted."

"I like my coffee sweet."

So saying he went to the canteen-counter and with a self-conscious expression began dropping lumps of sugar into his coffee. I stood by, watching him. When he had dropped in eight lumps he stopped and gave me a defiant stare. I stared back, levelly. He sighed and continued dropping lumps of sugar into his cup. The other lads gathered round to watch too. Finally the cup could hold no more sugar. The boy glared at me again. "You think I won't drink it, dontcher?"

"I've never said that."

"Well I like it this way, see?"

"Then you've a rapturous experience ahead of you," I said.

"Still betting I won't drink it?"

"Not at all. You like it that way. You've just said so. I believe you. So drink up."

"I bloody well will drink it too!" he bawled, furious with me.

"Of course," I purred.

The other boys joined in. "Go on, spoil yourself. You deserve a break. So go on, have some more sugar."

He glared at us once more a protracted, face-by-face glare, raised the cup, took two desperate gulps, shuddered violently, gave us another glare, saw our grins, tried another gulp, slammed down the cup and fled into the street. I never again found him pinching anything from the canteen.

In this manner we middle-aged squares contrived to run the Club during a very difficult period. Whether we dealt with our unclubables in a style of which professional pundits would approve I don't know. All I do know is that somehow we kept the Club open five nights a week and managed to avoid any real trouble. Only those who have attempted anything of this sort will know exactly what it means. It was a tough club, and we had a tough time with it, and somehow both the Club and ourselves survived.

CHAPTER XI

HAPPY CLUB

ONE OF OUR more ambitious projects during this period was an attempt to enter a group for a local Drama Festival. The play decided upon was what Chuck called "A Midnight Summer's Dream". He was unanimously chosen to play Bottom, a part with which he instantly became enchanted.

But Shakespeare was soon abandoned as "too fulla potry" and *The Dear Departed* was chosen instead. We held several rehearsals and had a lot of fun, although Chuck dropped out, claiming that acting was a waste of time. The fact was that he was disappointed at losing the chance to play Bottom.

The Dear Departed was getting along nicely and people were actually learning their parts when Hal approached the group waving an exercise-book and saying he'd written a smashing murder play. He read it to us; it was incredibly complicated, detectives, corpses and red-herrings proliferating like crazy. Every line of dialogue started with the word "Well." The only character I can recall was the grandmother, who was described as "old and withered, over forty." She had one unforgettable line, which she addressed to her grand-daughter, "Well, my girl, if you don't watch out you'll be feeling a high wind up your skirt."

The group didn't like the play. Nothing daunted Hal said that in that case he'd direct them in a smashing production of *The Monkey's Paw* instead. Unfortunately the contest was now only a week away and so, after all, our Club did nothing.

This was a disappointment. However, one gets hardened to disappointment when one does youth-work. One also becomes hardened to shocks; at least, one fancies that one has become so, but somehow there is always one more king-sized shock lurking round the corner.

One morning Mrs Z. telephoned me to say that she had driven past the Club at 2 a.m. that day and had been astounded to see that all the lights were on. A car had driven up, a man and a girl (strangers to Mrs Z.) had got out and had let themselves into the Club with a key that the girl had taken from her handbag. Mrs Z., thunderstruck, had then driven home.

"Why didn't you call the police?" I asked.

"Well, my dear, I did think of it, but on the other hand we don't want a thing like that in the newspapers. Think what a meal they'd make out of it."

I telephoned Mr N. to tell him the tale and ask him to put a new lock on the front-door. He said he would get a new lock on within a matter of a few hours. He added that he too had recently noticed lights at the Club early in the morning.

"But why on earth haven't you told me this before? It's a dreadfully serious matter. Suppose the county authority found out that we were passively sitting by while someone ran a . . . heaven knows what!"

"Precisely. Which is why I said nothing about it. A wretched tale for the newspapers to enjoy themselves with had the story leaked out," said Mr N. smugly.

We then had a most spirited conversation, to put it mildly. I shouted at him and he shouted at me. I felt that both he and Mrs Z. underrated the possible implications of the late-night-early-morning Club activities.

Someone had had a key or keys cut and the Club was being used as a late night snoggery, but enquiries failed to reveal any further information. Mrs X. and several neighbours had noticed lights but had not thought it any of their business. Sophie had recently been "sweeping up french letters galore off the floor in the mornings" but hadn't mentioned the matter because it wasn't a nice thing to talk about.

Mr N. had a mortice-lock on the door within hours of our telephone conversation. For this lock only two keys were cut, one of which was kept by Tim and the other by Sophie, who was instructed to report any dubious incidents in the future, however unpleasant.

Henceforth I was very much alert about Club security.

Slim, the bad boy who had gone in the Army and had made (comparatively speaking) good, was now killed in a road smash. Since he frequented our Club every time he returned on leave, our members contributed generously towards a wreath. Mrs Z. remarked rather bitterly upon their open-handedness on occasions of this sort and their tight-fistedness when it came to paying subs.

"They care about poor Slim," said Mr N. "They don't really care about the Club. Slim was one of them; the Club is just a place they come to, and a pretty crumby place at that."

"Oh, that's nonsense!" exclaimed Mrs Z. "How can you call this a crumby Club!"

"Just you go and look at some of these new youth-clubs that are being built," said Mr N. "Then come back here and tell me this place isn't crumby."

"It's the spirit of a youth-club that counts, not the state of the actual premises," replied Mrs Z.

However, we were trying to spruce up the premises before a new Leader arrived. We had already applied for grant-aid to buy wallpapers, paint and so on.

Mr N. offered to get us some paint cheaply. Delighted, we asked him to get us as much as he could. In due course several large tins of paint arrived. They were all eau-de-nil.

When Tim showed me I was aghast. "What on earth can Mr N. be thinking of, getting us eau-de-nil?"

"Don't you like eau-de-nil, Madam Chairman?" asked Tim.

"Eau-de-nil," I replied, bitterly, "is only fit for crocodiles." This remark unfortunately reached the ears of Mr N. who, it transpired, was very fond of eau-de-nil. He never forgave me. We no longer saw him at the Club and he sent me a stiff note asking for his paint back.

Unhappily we could not return it. Some of it was already on the walls and the remainder had mysteriously vanished. Pretty obviously one of our young villains had whipped it.

A further foolish and frigid correspondence passed between Mr N. and myself. Finally he resigned from the Management Committee.

He was, in point of fact, a very sick man and almost immediately upon his resignation he had to go into hospital for a series of severe operations from which he never recovered. Had he been in his usual state of health I do not think he would have quarrelled with us over eau-de-nil paint.

It was March again; spring winds blew down our straight and narrow street, past the chipped spastic child and the courting cats that crouched all eyes and twitching whiskers, under the sooty privet hedges. A wind of change; upon it arrived our new Leader.

The Management Committee had requested that the next full-time Leader should be a strong leader with experience. The

Youth Office people had agreed. Now, four months after Skip's departure, came a new, strong, experienced Leader. We virtually fell upon him.

He was certainly immensely fit, trim, brisk, authoritative. He had earned himself a first-class reputation at his previous clubs, which had all been boys' clubs in pretty tough districts.

He had no time for record-appreciation or film-making and I doubt that he had heard of Pinter. His first request, upon arrival, was for more gym equipment and a new billiard-table.

He obviously thought a woman chairman a pretty rum idea, too.

The reaction of the Club members to the new Leader was mixed. A few immediately welcomed his firm handling while others disliked him, complaining that we had fetched in a Hearty as a Leader. The footballers and weight-trainers watched him narrowly. Then Hal summed him up in one terse word, "Shtorika."* Chuck didn't even put his verdict into speech; realizing that his day of authority at the Club was over he joined the Merchant Navy.

"Gonna get outa this dump and see the world," he explained.

"See something of the birds of other lands, eh mate?" said Hal. "Roving bird-fancier, like."

"Yeah, bird in every port," said Fred.

"Thatsa life," said Chuck.

"Well I hope you're not tied up with anyone back home here," I said, "for it would be unfair to her and a perishing bore for you."

"Don't worry, Mrs B., I got rid of all my steadies. My reg'lar bird, I told her, I don't want nobody mopin' about at home waiting for letters what never come an' all that jazz. I want that free, roamin' feeling. You can take my word I bin careful to cut all me what d'you call 'ems . . . ties."

"Musta took you several weeks' hard work, mate," said Hal, "seeing that you had a real good supply of what-d'you-call-'ems to cut."

"Comin' to the end of the list now, mate," said Chuck.

I encountered him one evening very shortly after this, rather drunk, ambling along the High Street after closing-time with his arm round a buxom little lass with long ringlets. She too was comfortably sloshed. They were lurching amiably along, tightly

* Shtorika: a strong-armed man.

entwined, heads close together, singing with completely innocent, indeed gentle expressions on their faces, like two inebriated
cherubs. Chuck never noticed me. He was totally absorbed in
his singing and his song-bird. Clearly, cutting his ties was a
pleasurable process.

Finally he came to say a last good-bye to us at the Club.

"Look in and tell us about your adventures when you get
back," I said.

"I hope they'll be the sort what I can't tell you about, duck,"
he replied. And away he went, bound for Singapore.

We now had sixty-three members; thirty-seven boys and
twenty-six girls. Of the boys twenty-two were over fifteen years
of age and fifteen under. Six of the girls were over fifteen,
twenty under. The six senior girls were Edwina, Petunia, Sally,
Sue, Dee (only just fifteen) and a small, dark newcomer, Morag.

The Club at this period was very mixed in every sense. About
half our members were the "O" level taking, sharply dressed,
responsive and at least in some degree socially responsible
young people who would later be labelled Mods. The rest were
leather-jacketed, motor-bike mounted, skidlidded, juke-box
playing, rebellious young toughs, the incipient Rocks.

Upon the whole these two groups were, when in the Club,
quite well integrated.

During these spring and early summer months our Management Committee membership underwent change. The evangeli-
cally minded people had by now all left and the last of the Cubes
also departed. We filled their places with as many efficient,
hard-headed, warm-hearted, experienced people as we could;
avoiding anybody who wished to save, uplift, or do good works
amongst the young. We looked for people who liked teen-agers
and would enjoy helping to evolve a successful club for them.
By successful club we meant a club that young people would
enjoy coming to.

I am sometimes asked what a youth-club aims to achieve if it
eschews uplift, rescue and good works. Well, it provides a
meeting-place for young people who would otherwise congre-
gate on street-corners. It provides a place of regular refuge
from unhappy or otherwise unsatisfactory homes. It should try
to broaden the horizons of its members (which I suppose is a
species of uplift) and, above all, the Leaders and other adults
there can offer uncritical, loyal friendship to the members. A

5

boy, for instance, can be not only sure of a smile and a welcome if he comes back to the club after, say, a time away training with the sea-cadets, likewise he can be equally sure of a smile and a welcome if he returns to the club after a spell in Borstal. Whenever he comes into the club (unless, of course, he is on the run and dodges in to use the place as an alibi, or is seeking refuge from a rival gang that pounds in, hot on his heels, brandishing knives and coshes) there is a friendly smile waiting for him. This is really terribly important.

When a member comes from a good and happy home the club is just one more pleasant place to go to and may be quite easily dispensed with, but in numbers of instances the club is the only pleasant place to go to. Mum has gone off with another chap, dad drinks, and home is a cheerless prefab. Under circumstances such as these a youth-club can be vital to a boy or girl. If a club Leader can win the confidence and affection of the members, he or she, may be able to give these young people real help with their problems.

Our Leader was anxious to expand our weight-training group and asked if he might build an annexe to house the equipment. He received the go-ahead to do this. At this juncture Rory returned from Borstal. He asked to resume Club membership. He was duly readmitted and, since he was a natural handyman (when not out to be intentionally obstructive or destructive) we employed him upon building the annexe, for which of course he was paid the correct wage. In this way we hoped to help the boy find his feet during the always difficult first weeks following release from any of H.M. establishments of detention.

Rory settled down to the job very well; he was co-operative, polite, hard-working.

Tim W. left us; Bonny C. returned.

Our first major enterprise after the Leader's arrival was another jumble-sale.

Collecting the stuff was more soberly done this time; I had no hilarious evenings with Midge and Gavin. The highlight of my door-to-door work was an encounter with a vitriolic old man, who, upon hearing that I was collecting for a youth-club, spat at me, "Madam, I'd rather *eat* my jumble than give it to a youth-club!" And he slammed the door in my face.

Senior members made an especially good effort, collecting

jumble nightly during the week before the sale and sorting the stuff and putting it out on stalls and pricing it the morning of the day of the sale. In the afternoon they turned out in force to sell; many of them in fancy costumes contrived from the various items of clothing on the stalls. It was the time when Acker Bilk was the rage and several had dressed themselves in waistcoats and bowlers. Hal wore a white dress-waistcoat and a huge flowered cravat, Fred a white linen cap, black bow-tie and a white waistcoat several times too large for him. Clem had a hat that made him look like a cross between Nehru and an American tourist. Rory had equipped himself with a bowler, a red waistcoat and a magnificently rolled civil-servant type umbrella which he carried dangling over his arm all afternoon.

Everyone was busy, relaxed and happy. We made just over twenty pounds; pretty successful for us.

The Leader, as everyone said, had got away to a swimming start. At the A.G.M., held a week or two after the jumble-sale, the Leader said that we could look forward with some confidence to a successful year. I said that the Club had survived its difficult patch and could now forge ahead with confidence into what I was certain would be a bright future. These cliché-ridden prophecies having been uttered, the members performed a short one-act play and gave a P.T. display. We had sent invitations to sixty-odd parents; four turned up.

Rory had been appointed a steward for the evening; such was the esteem in which we now held him. He arrived half-way through the programme, rolling-drunk, and tried to fight the Leader. He was suspended from the Club for a fortnight.

At the end of the fortnight he was back. In an obvious effort to reinstate himself in our good books he applied himself zealously to redecorating the committee-room. I discovered him doing some dainty stippling work on the door. "Hello Rory. You're doing that very tastefully."

"Yeah, nice, innit? I'm gonna get a stained-glass effect, like in a church, you know?"

Fred was busy collecting contributions towards the Outings Fund. He scurried round the Club rattling the Oxo tin. The first outing, he told me, was to be a day-trip to Boulogne.

He approached Bertie, one of our newest members; a thick-faced, tousle-headed, gruff-voiced, inarticulate sixteen-year old. Bertie said, "Boulogne; wheresat mate?"

"France, mush."

"I ain't going to France, tosh."

"Come on, we all going. Be fun. Come on, pay your whack."

"No bloody likely, mate. Eat snails an' sick 'em all up on the way 'ome? Bleedin' funny way of having fun."

"You're ignorant, thass your trouble. Come on mate; do you good. Travel broadens the mind."

"How can he broaden his mind, mate?" sang out Rory. "Got no bleedin' mind to broaden."

The piqued Bertie responded, "Rather 'ave no bleedin' mind to broaden, mate, than bugger it up with snails an' frogs."

Twelve senior members went, in the end. They drank Byrrh, under the impression that it was beer, did the Palais Glide along the sea-front and were, as Bertie had forecast, horribly sick coming back.

Rory returned with a crab which he had caught on the beach. On arrival home he placed it in a bucket of water in which he emptied a packet of table-salt, but in spite of this attention it died.

"Pity, that. I'da liked a real French crab," said Rory. "Mattera fack, iffita lived, I was gonna give it you, Mrs B., seein' how you're part French an' all. Thought you'da liked it as a souvenir."

"A terribly nice thought, even though it didn't come off," I said.

"It wasa wrong kinda salt, I bet," interjected Bertie.

"Sifta," said Rory.

"Runny or block?"

"Runny."

"Shoulda bin block," said Bertie, " 's stronger. Sea's fuckin' salt, mate."

The Leader then appeared and terminated the conversation.

The next outing was a week-end trip to Herne Bay. Bertie was keen to go on this one, but could not afford the whole cost of the trip. The Management Committee agreed to help finance him. We expected no thanks; we were long past the stage when we expected thanks. Imagine our surprise then when a week after the trip we received a letter from the boy, expressing his appreciation!

He also approached me and thanked me verbally. I said I was glad that he had enjoyed himself so much. His chunky face broke into an immensely wide grin; embarrassed, he wiped back his greasy hair with a nicotine-stained hand; "It was smashin'."

The adults who had gone with the party confirmed that it had been a very good week-end, though there had been some trouble keeping one unofficially engaged couple from unofficially consummating their unofficially plighted troth. "When they were on the beach they kept rolling away under a breakwater and when they got back indoors they kept nipping up to the bedrooms," said the Leader. "But we successfully frustrated 'em. At least, I think we did. I couldn't vouch for when they were actually in the water."

The Club was now obviously going through a happy period. Our new Leader had lifted us out of a state of aggressive chaos arising from a regime of *laissez-faire* and had reintroduced order and control to just the right degree. The young people knew where they stood and young people very much like, indeed require to know, where they stand. Otherwise they become confused and confusion leads them into trouble.

Our members enjoyed the discipline, the full list of activities, the week-end outings and so forth. These things no longer came haphazardly, but were part of a carefully worked-out programme. Membership still stood at sixty-five, but the average nightly attendance had increased from thirty-five to forty-five. We were still a very small club, but nonetheless we were a successful club. The Leader planned a recruiting-drive in the autumn. Meantime his principal aim was consolidation.

It was interesting to see that some half-dozen or so of our younger former boys now rejoined the Club, amongst them Gavin and Midge.

In June we arranged for sex-talks to be given at the Club by a woman doctor. She made two visits; the first time simply to chat with the members and get to know them a little, the second time to give the talks.

The girls openly admitted to a need for sex-instruction; they explained that they could not discuss sex with their mothers. But the boys wouldn't admit to any need for instruction; it seemed that they knew it all. However they indicated that they would attend the talks purely out of courtesy to the doctor. "Don't want the poor old geezer talkin' to empty air." For her sake they would hear what she had to say.

The only two members who refused point-blank to attend the talks were the Club's leading wolves; Hal and Tug. I could see their point-of-view; they, who claimed to be complete experts, would lose face badly if they attended a sex-talk.

Tug was a fairly new member; thin, large-featured, edgy, with a sense of humour that failed when himself became the target. He dressed very sharply, favouring mohair zipped sweaters (then the last word in switched-on masculine attire) in eye-searing emerald-greens, parma-violets and lemon-yellows. His stacked-heeled winkle-pickers would have opened a can of baked-beans. Although he never appeared to be enjoying mad success with the actual girls at the Club his talk was all of the birds who flocked, but flocked to him.

Hal's reputation for conquest could hardly have been founded on his Club activities either, so far as I could see (admittedly one never can see very far in these matters; seldom so far as one fondly thinks). But the girls related to one another innumerable anecdotes about his sex-life at week-ends. These made him sound a veritable Don Juan.

On the other hand Hal was a writer. He actually handed me sixty-minute T.V. plays to read. The writer's job is not one that leaves him (or her) with unlimited time for bed. Writing, as writers themselves are forever proclaiming, is a lonely craft. One can't make love *and* bash a typewriter. Togetherness is out, for authors. I knew, from bitter first-hand experience, that Hal must spend a lot of time alone in his room getting all that dialogue on to paper.

Be that as it may, Hal and Tug had wolfish reputations; to them sex was no mystery (or so they incessantly claimed). Now they paraded round the Club breathing scorn: "Sex talks, huh? Birds an' bees an' all that jazz, huh? How the flowers do it." I was afraid that they might put the rest of the kids off the talks too, but they didn't.

The doctor on her first, purely social, visit went down well with the members. On her second visit she had a preliminary cup of coffee in the canteen and then started a session, first with the girls, in the powder-room; we felt this was an informal, easier place for the talks than, say the committee-room.

Tug watched the girls go into the powder-room. He then ordered a coke from me and as he sipped it said, "What's an old bag like her know about sex anyway?"

The doctor was middle-aged.

I said, "She's a doctor and a married woman and, though you wouldn't know it, pretty distinguished in her own line. And when you reach her age I doubt you'll think of yourself as senile. And finally, what do you really know about sex yourself?"

"Ask my birds, they'll tell you," leered Tug.

Presently the girls came out and the boys went in. The girls, I thought, looked unusually pensive. I had rather expected them to come out giggling, but they didn't.

Bonny, who had attended the talk with them, came into the canteen to have a cup of coffee with me and said that the doctor had a wonderful way with young people.

Hal and Tug meantime eyed the other boys squeezing into the powder-room. They themselves assumed expressions suited to men of vast experience, but presently they both repaired to the canteen, ordered coffees and began.

"Here, what's she gonna tell 'em, Mrs B.?"

"Go and listen for yourselves. Then you'll know, won't you?"

"Yeah, buttercups and daisies."

Pause.

"What's she gonna say to 'em, Mrs B.?"

"She's telling them about sex."

"Yeah, but what about it? Come on, Mrs B. You must know what she's telling 'em."

"Look, she's the one who's giving the talk, not me. You go and listen to her. She's a distinguished woman and well worth listening to."

"Oh sure. All that crap 'bout birds and bees."

"Since you know it all so well, why come and ask me what she's telling them?"

"Tadpoles, how they turn into frogs."

"I'm quite certain she isn't talking about tadpoles."

"What's she talkin' about then?"

"Go and listen. Find out," said Bonny.

"Found all that out years ago," said Tug.

He and Hal turned their backs on us and eyed the powder-room door wistfully. Obviously they were both dying to attend the talks. Equally obviously they dared not risk serious loss of face. Everyone knew that they knew it all.

The girls now descended on the canteen, chattering and

laughing; clearly recovered a little from the sobering effects of learning the unvarnished facts of life. They ordered cokes and coffees. Then out came the boys from the powder-room. They jostled up to the canteen too. Dee shouted at them, "Hey, what she tell you?"

Pete roared back, "To lay off silly little gels like you!"

"Yeah, she says it's silly little birds like you what lands chaps like us in trouble!" bawled Bertie.

The girls were deeply affronted. "Why, what's wrong with us?" they shrieked in unison.

"You're silly, ignorant, don't know nothing. Get us into trouble; she says so," replied Clem. "She says to lay right off you."

"Ignorant!" squealed Petunia. "I like that. We know the lot now, thanks to her."

"Yeah, we know it all now," chimed in Morag. "She jus' told us."

"All?" jeered Hal.

"Yeah, all've it," repeated Morag, lowering her eyelids, which that evening were painted bright cobalt-blue. "Littel babies an' the lot."

"We're experts now Tug, same as you!" shrilled Dee. Tug bawled back, "It's practice what makes perfeck, mate!"

However it gradually transpired from conversations which the Leader, Bonny and I overheard and upon which we compared notes that the sex-talks had not only been very much needed, gently enlightening several bemused minds, but that they had also done a good deal of good so far as Club behaviour went. Far from encouraging sexual activity amongst the Club members, the talks had had an opposite effect. The Club had been passing through a definite period of sexual excitement (this had been one of the reasons why I had suggested the talks, there is nothing like a shower of cold, objective scientific facts to cool the fevered imagination). For the first time in their lives the members had been asked to stand back and talk and think about sex intelligently, without prejudice or emotion. If young people *are* going to carry out sex experiments together in dark alleyways, or under dusty bushes in twilit public parks, they should at least be given the benefit of knowing exactly what they are doing, and what is the likely outcome.

There are many people who will hasten to point out that sex

is something much more than a physical act, that it carries deep emotional and social significance. Indeed it does. But, in the context of our Club, sex meant, purely and simply, the screwing of a bird by a boy. The problem had to be dealt with upon that level. It is foolish to imbue a problem with more significance than it naturally carries within itself. To have built up the sex problem at our Club into something complicated and loaded would have been, let us say, like walking up Parliament Hill burdened with gear designed for the Matterhorn.

Of course I am not contending that, after the sex-talks, all sex activity came to an end amongst our Club members, but we no longer noticed the sexually overheated atmosphere such as there had been at the Club for a brief period.

Doubtless a contributing factor to the improved state of affairs was the departure of Dolly. She had become avid for boys and her avidity had been highly infectious.

It was interesting to observe that Dee, bereft of her mate Dolly, had dropped her interest in boys and now made twisting her major addiction. She spent the greater part of every evening twisting, solo, slap up against the juke-box. Every now and then she would break off to refresh herself with a cigarette and a coke, perhaps she would nip into the powder-room to relacquer her hair; then back she would come to start twisting again. Her trooper-like invective was reserved solely for those persons who turned off the juke-box while she was in mid-twist.

The time had now arrived for what was gaily known as the Southend Walk. This "walk" had been instigated by Skip two summers previously. It was fifty miles from our Club to Southend and the walking was done overnight when the roads were empty; the idea of getting away from the roads was something that never crossed the minds of these children of the automobile age. Besides, to date, the "walk" had always been accomplished, for the last thirty miles, in a van.

Twenty miles is quite a decent stint for people who normally never walk anywhere and who should, logically, have been born with wheels instead of feet, but it is a far cry from fifty miles.

The Club members now made their annual application to the Management Committee for petrol for the Southend Walk. I asked to see the boys who were actually planning the expedition. Fred, Clem, Pete and Rory presented themselves.

5*

"What's this petrol for?" I asked.

"Why, the van."

"What's the van for?"

"To pick up stragglers."

"I thought this was a walk?"

"Yeah, but you need a van for stragglers, dontcher?"

"Why?"

"Well, 'sobvious, innit?"

"No, it's not."

"Stone it, whatcha do with the blokes what drop out too tired to go on?"

"Leave them to lie by the roadside until they feel fit to get up and carry on with the walk," I said. "The weather's nice and warm; nobody's going to die of exposure this time of the year."

There was an appalled silence. Then Fred began, "But . . ."

"Look," I said, "every year you lot talk about the Southend Walk. But what you really mean is a Southend Ride. The Management Committee, and the Leader, are fed up with big talk about a walk and then what it boils down to is a ride in a van. Why not be honest and say you want petrol money for the annual Southend Ride?"

" 's fifty miles," murmured Fred. "You ever walk fifty miles, Mrs B.?"

"To be honest, I have not. The most I ever walked at one stretch is thirty-four miles, but that was in the Lake District, over hills of two thousand to three thousand feet. The equivalent of that, in terms of estimated expenditure of energy, on the flat, is round about sixty-eight miles. Of course I agree it is much more fun walking in hilly country; you don't notice distances so much. Would you like us to have a walking weekend in the Lake District together? Do a thirty mile walk up there instead of a fifty-mile walk down here, perhaps?"

They looked at me. God knows what they really thought of me. At last Rory said, "Orright, we'll walk to Southend this year without the van."

However the Leader and I were finally persuaded (no doubt correctly) by the Treasurer and Secretary that we must have a van to pick up stragglers because parents might complain if their exhausted offspring were left to lie all night in a ditch. It was decided, however, that the van should travel slowly, some distance behind the walkers, well out of their sight. In this way its bad psychological effect upon them would be at least somewhat mitigated.

Several of the girls had at first declared their intention of doing the "walk", but now that they heard the boys speaking of doing the entire fifty miles without a van they lost interest.

There was a move to get both the Leader and myself on the walk; to see if we were really capable of it, I have no doubt. Mrs Z. said to me, "D'you really think you could do it, Mary?"

"Yes, I could *do* it. What I'd be like next day is another matter; but I reckon I could just about do it. Stagger down on to Southend beach and collapse into the cooling arms of the ocean."

Still, the Leader and I were not put to the test. It was decided that things would be more fun without us. The Leader was left to drive the van and I was told that all I need do was to wish them luck when they started.

Fred went round the Club getting recruits for the walk. His powers of persuasion were considerable; I listened to his sales-talk, as it were, with interest. He got Midge and Gavin to agree to go, and Mike, and a newcomer named Lance. He was just signing up Lance when Bertie strolled up. Dear Bertie. Fred asked him if he would walk to Southend?"

"Whatsa good? Won't be no fun with 'im there," said Bertie.

"With who there?"

"Perishin' Leader. I know 'im. If you wanta go behind a bush with a bird, he'll stop you, an' if you wanta swear, he'll stop you. He can't let you 'ave no fun, nothing for a giggle, that bloke."

Bertie and the Leader had been having a bit of an up-and-down over unpaid subs. Hence the disgruntlement.

"There won't be any time for sessions with birds," I said, "and as for swearing, surely you can manage without that for a few hours?"

"No. I like to swear," said Bertie, plaintively.

"Well, I tell you what. When you feel you want to swear, run ahead, out of earshot of the rest, have a good old swear on your own so the Leader can't hear you and then nip back and join the rest of the party. Nobody will mind that," I said.

"Yeah, that's the way to do it, Bertie," said Fred. "I'll put you down for the walk."

" 'ow many miles?"

"Fifty, Bertie boy. You'll do it easy."

"Fifty bleedin' miles! Stone it! Who was the perisher thoughta that?"

"Don't matter who it was. You're gonna walk fifty miles, tosh."

The night of July 20 – 21st was fixed as the date of the walk. Ten boys were ready at the Club to depart at 8 p.m.; blasting-off time, as Rory said. The party consisted of Fred, Clem, Lance, Mike, Bertie, Hal, Midge, Gavin, Pete and Rory.

At the last moment an eleventh walker turned up; Rory's fourteen-year-old cousin, Winston. He was not a Club member, but expressed a passionate desire to walk to Southend.

We looked at him anxiously. "Will he make it?" asked the Leader.

"If he don't I'll have his bleedin' liver out," replied Rory genially. So Winston was allowed to join the walk.

I had sent them a good-luck telegram, like the ones you send theatre-friends on their first-nights. I think the boys all felt a trifle first-nightish as they stood waiting to start.

On the stroke of eight it began to pour with rain. It was still sluicing down when they marched off. Their departure in such weather was sufficient alone to do them credit. Not one of them had brought a mac.

Shortly after starting Midge had to retire because the heel of his shoe came off.

Of the remaining ten walkers five made it to Southend. These five were Clem (in spite of fearful blisters), Gavin, Lance, Rory and his cousin Winston. Poor Fred, in an agony from blisters, gave up twelve miles outside Southend. Bertie also had to give up because of the state of his feet; after thirty-two miles. He was so loath to retire from his attempt that he had to be forcibly lifted, kicking, swearing and weeping into the van. Pete and Hal gave up after they had gone twenty miles. Mike retired at fifteen. He never quite forgave himself for this.

Rory, on arrival at Southend, revealed a horribly swollen right ankle and explained that he had twisted it, falling down-stairs, the previous day. He had said nothing about it until now as he had feared that the Leader might not let him attempt the walk. "But I got to Southend on it, mate. Don't mind if they amputate it now."

None of these boys had put in any training for the walk. Rory, however, did observe that he was pretty fit because he had just come out of Borstal. "You do a lotta prancin' about at Borstal."

Everyone at the Club was terribly proud of their walkers and the local paper carried a picture of the triumphant five and a story.

A week later the Club had another triumph; this time at the Swimming Gala. We retained the shield which, the reader will remember, we had won the previous summer under rather dubious circumstances. The means by which we retained it were, I fear, equally reprehensible.

The Management Committee this year, bearing in mind the events of the previous year, vowed that Gala rules must be rigidly observed. Contestants, said these rules, must belong to a youth organization and be under the age of twenty-one. A Club team had to consist of paid-up members from that club.

Our team was being painfully assembled when back came Chuck on shore-leave from the Merchant Navy. He looked in at the Club on his first evening home and paid a visitor's subscription. He was asked, by Fred, if he would be available to captain the Gala swimming-team and replied that he would love to. The question of Club membership was queried; Chuck flung money carelessly on to the canteen-counter and said he would pay any sub money we asked for. The Vice-Chairman asked if Chuck were not nearing the age-limit? Chuck gave one of his toothy, marvellously happy-making smiles and declared that that was all orright.

So Chuck led our team and with his accomplished swimming and diving was largely instrumental, as he had been the previous year, on our team winning every event they entered. And so we kept our lovely shield.

An evening or so later, when we were all in the canteen drinking coffees and talking, Rory remarked casually that old Chuck must be coming up for twenty-five this summer, or was it twenty-six?

"Twenty-six!" cried the Vice-Chairman and I, in horror.

"Twenty-five jus' come up, act'lly," said Chuck, with one of his particularly disarming grins.

"But you should have left the Club years ago! My dear Chuck, you should never have even joined the Club in the first place!" I said. "You were over-age before you started."

"Always did look a lot younger than me years," said Chuck,

adding aggrievedly, "An' why couldn't I belong to this Club? Arter all, you didn't want me on the streets, did you?"

"One thing emerges very clearly from all this," said the Leader. "From what you people have told me, you had no right to that damn shield last year, and now we've no right to it this year, either."

"Do we hand it back?" asked Bonny.

"Good grief no," said the Vice-Chairman. "We're simply running true to form."

"All said an' done, I didn't swim for my own glory. I swam for the honour of the Club," said Chuck.

After he had ambled off to do a little weight-training I said, "I always did consider that boy wonderfully mature for his age."

"Don't harp on it, Mary," said the Vice-Chairman. "He's probably a grandfather, if we but knew it. Should, by rights, belong to the Darby and Joan Club."

"And there was that poor chairman of the Youth Committee congratulating our team on winning the shield and saying what a wonderful effort it was for a Club like ours to have a team like that," said Bonny.

"It's only a club like ours that *could* have a team like that," said the Vice-Chairman.

PART FOUR

MOMENTS OF TRUTH

CHAPTER XII

A WINTER'S TALE

WE HAD NOT survived more than a few weeks of our new autumn session before a great change took place in the Club membership. The footballers had, for some time, been carrying on a running debate with the Leader about their finances. They claimed that any money that they raised, by dances, raffles and so forth, belonged to their team and not to the Club. We maintained that the football-team was simply part of the Club as a whole and that all the money raised by the team should be handed over to swell the general Club funds. This Hal and his football mates simply would not, or could not, see.

They spent hours discussing the matter with me. Personally I sought to work for a good old British compromise, but the Leader, who naturally had more to say in the matter than I had, became thoroughly fed up with them and finally turned them out of the Club.

It was true that they were rude and aggressive in their behaviour towards authority, it was true that they were inclined to be loutish towards the girls, wolf-whistling and passing loud, embarrassing remarks (though whether the girls honestly minded this I don't know). It was true, too, that all the footballers were round the twenty mark and would soon have been leaving us anyway (since the Chuck episode we had become rather more alert to age limits than hitherto). Nevertheless striking problem members off a youth-club subscription list is never a very satisfactory solution. Still, the Leader took the line that the footballers were troublemakers and that the Club was better off without them and, after all, he was the man to decide.

Hal, of course, departed with them. Tug, Pete and Rory left too, in sympathy. In this manner we found ourselves with only three really senior boys remaining; Fred, Clem and Mike.

In the place of the departed seniors came several new members, nearly all sixteen-year old Mod types. Indeed we had virtually become a club for young Mods (the term, Mod, was now coming into vogue). Although we still had a small Rock element, of both sexes, this played a very subsidiary Club role.

It must be emphasized that our Mod element was not a switched-on, King's Road Mod element, sophisticated and sexy, but a lower-middle-class outer-outer-suburban Mod element. Mid really, rather than Mod. Or, as one of the girls described it, "Mod-Mid."

These Mods of ours tried hard to copy the switched-on, way-out London Mods, but they lacked that little extra essential something that marks the difference, say, between a Courrèges model and a copy in the local High Street.

Some of our Mods were, of course, intelligent, charming young people who made good, stimulating company, but then they would have been all that at any time, any place and with whatever kind of label they had chosen to wear. But some of the others were decidedly grotty, especially the little Mod girls.

More and more of these little moddy birds now joined the Club and frankly one sometimes wondered why they bothered to. Once inside they sat round like zombies, occasionally getting up to indulge in some lackadaisical twisting. We had been anxious to recruit little birds in order to attract younger boys who would, in due course, graduate to replace our departed seniors, but these birds wouldn't have attracted an emasculated swiss-roll, as Mike commented.

"You're dead right mate. They're wet, right wet," said Stoker, a new sixteen-year-old member who was neither Rock nor Mod but his own ebullient, inimitable self.

Bonny suggested that we might make the girls more exciting to the boys by the simple expedient of making them rather more inaccessible. "I once worked at a club, you know, where we had a girls' common-room; boys were only allowed in by invitation. It was amazing; the boys used to queue up to get asked in."

So part of our large entrance-hall, adjoining the powder-room, was partitioned off to make a girls' common-room. The little birds filed demurely into it and sat down on the contemporary metal-and-plastic chairs with which we had temptingly furnished it. They showed not the slightest desire to invite any of the boys to join them; instead they brought loads of pictures of Cliff Richard, Adam Faith, Elvis Presley, Tommy Steele and Billy Fury, and in due course the Beatles, and papered the walls with these. Meantime the boys went cheerfully about their various activities, revealing for their part not the slightest interest in the inmates of the pop-star plastered common-room.

"Don't any of you lads want a session in there with those girls?" queried the Leader.

"Session of doin' what, guv?"

"Why, dance, talk," said the Leader.

"With them wets?"

"Can't make you lot out. When I was your age I wouldn't have left a group of girls like that to their own devices all evening. I'd've been in there, asking for a dance, trying to fix a date or two."

Clem muttered to me, "He musta bin hard up for birds, that geezer, if he had to fall back on a loada twits like that."

"This sex-crazy generation you read about in the newspapers, where is it?" sighed Bonny.

"Comes and goes in pockets," said the Vice-Chairman. "This time last year, when you were nursing your slipped-disc, Mrs B. and I were spending our evenings breaking up sex-orgies behind the pianos."

"They were a different lot, though, from this bunch we've got down here now," I said.

"A different lot altogether. And in some ways, oddly enough, much easier to get along with," said the Vice-Chairman.

The Leader and I had arranged to follow up the sex-talks of the previous session with a talk on V.D., the talk to be specially geared for teen-agers and given by the M.O.H.

The M.O.H. was keen to give the talk, but he asked me to soften his audience up a bit first for him, as he put it. "I don't want to talk to them cold. Get them ready with questions and so forth."

So the Leader and I held a preliminary session with the Members' Committee; Sue, Morag, Sally, Petunia, Fred, Don (a new boy who was doing his D. of E. silver award) and Ian (another new member, an avid weight-trainer). This was an almost entirely Mod committee.

They listened politely while I explained about the proposed talks. What did they think of the idea?

There was a long silence. Then Fred said, "Not necessary."

"Maybe not for you," I said, "but surely you're not suggesting that all the members of this Club are in a similarly well-informed state?"

"I don't mean that," said Fred. "I don't say that they are, at all. But I mean it's not necessary, that sort of talk, because hardly none of 'em will bother to turn up to hear it."

"Why not?"

"Because they won't want to hear it," said Morag.

"Again, why not?"

"Don't interest 'em," said Ian.

There was another pause. Then Sue said, very kindly and sweetly, "Well, I hope you won't mind me saying this, Mrs B., but you see our lot's just not as interested in sex as you are."

This was a real hand-out.

"Your generation makes more of it than we do, you know?" said Morag.

I could hear the Leader breathing somewhat stertorously beside me. I said, in what I hoped was too a kind and sweet voice, "That may possibly be the case, but nonetheless sex is one of those things that does hit pretty well everybody in some degree or the other before they're through."

"We know that, Mrs B., but us lot mostly come from big families and we get to know about sex without keep on having to harp on it," said Don.

"That may be true too, but coming from a big family doesn't automatically mean you're well-informed on these things. Besides, the talk the M.O.H. plans to give isn't an ordinary sex-talk, it's about venereal disease. And he wants to give you lot this talk because, let's face it, thousands of teen-agers do get venereal disease, and it's therefore something that people in your age-group certainly should know something about."

They stared at me gloomily.

"I think we know all we need to know at this stage, Mrs B.," said Ian at last, still with this marvellous, patient courtesy, as though talking to a rather alien form of life; something a bit strange that had stepped out of a space-craft, perhaps. He added with just a shade more heat, "I mean, it isn't as if we're all rushin' out to go mad on sex, or something."

"I'm not suggesting that you are. But surely you'll agree that the more you know of facts, any facts, the better you will be able to deal with the problems of actual life when they hit you? Because life will hit you in the end, I do assure you, and I don't want you to meet these things absolutely green."

"Learn about 'em when the time comes," cooed Morag, soothingly.

"Well," said the Leader, "all I know is that when I was your age, I would have been most relieved to have met someone with Mrs B's attitude."

"Your lot was different," said Morag, with that same patient kindness. "You were sorta hedged-round like, so you were bothered more. You were frustrated more, so you thought about it more. We're just not so taken up by sex as you all were."

"It's not such a king-sized hoo-ha thing for us as it was for you," chimed in Sue.

"Well," said the Leader lamely, "if any of you do feel worried about anything, just remember that Mrs B. and I are at hand to give any help or advice that we can."

And then the two of us fled to his office to recover over a couple of coffees.

"By gum!" he said. "That was ripe."

"Why, what happened?" asked Bonny. We told her. She listened with her eyes opening and her lips twitching, then she started to giggle. "Hedged about? What, our lot hedged about? In the Services, in the middle of a war?"

"Enough to make a cat laugh, isn't it?" said the Leader, grinning reminiscently.

"They haven't a clue, have they?" mused Bonny, also with a rather enigmatic smile.

"No," I said. "Not a ruddy clue."

The Leader pulled himself together. "We shouldn't be talking like this, Madam Chairman."

"One has to talk about it, to try to get it sorted out. Actually the hedged-round lot were the lot before us; the lot D. H. Lawrence was writing for."

"Which reminds me," said Bonny. "Mike came in the other evening with a copy of *Lady Chatterley*; he said his English master had advised him to read it, because it was such an important book. You know? So I asked Mike what he thought of it."

"And?"

"He said that it was a grotty lot of codswallop."

"There you are. At least they've got that sort of thing out of their systems."

"It's a rum old way of life, is youth-work," said the Leader, lighting us all cigarettes. We had decided that adults should give up smoking on Club premises as an example to the young, but this evening had proved such a strain that we felt we might make it an exception.

"Consider, though," I said, "if somebody had written a report on the sexual behaviour of teen-agers based on the lot we had down here last year they would have drawn conclusions that would have made the public's hair stand up on end. Whereas now, at the mention of the word sex, this lot reprimand *us*."

"These are the grammar-stream children," said Bonny. "They've got socially acceptable ambitions and a reasonable chance of achieving them. But the other lot were mostly non-grammar-stream and socially horribly frustrated. They knew, poor little souls, that they could never hope to get anywhere. So they and their like fall back on sexual goals of attainment since they've failed in the world of exams and accepted social progress. They've all decided to make a name for themselves as rebels, failing all else."

"Sounds convincing," said the Leader.

"Take Dolly, for instance," said Bonny, warming to her theme. "She couldn't get O-levels, couldn't even get her eleven-plus, so she decided to compensate by having as many boys as she could. Prove to us that she could do something."

"Maybe she just enjoyed doing it and was out to have a hell of a good time," I said.

"You don't go to enough basic-training courses for youth-leaders, Madam Chairman," said the Leader.

"We must never forget," said Bonny, not to be put off her social theorizing by us, "that joining this Club is, in itself, a gesture of rebellion. Even our better-type members are obviously in a state of rebellion, however slight, against the adult world; else they would have joined a nicer sort of club, more the sort of club their parents would approve of, you know?"

"Well," said the Leader, rising, "whether they're in a state of rebellion or not they've all got to pack up and go home now, for it's ten o'clock and I'm going to close the Club."

Stoker now proceeded to balance the Mod influence at the Club by introducing his mate, Carrots, as a member. Carrots was a keen amateur boxer, earthy in his outlook, anything but moddy.

Carrots and Stoker confided to me that it was their joint ambition to go whaling. They went to the Iceland Travel

Bureau and made enquiries; they were told that they were too young and not physically strong enough yet to join the crew of a whaler. As a first step towards the goal of great physical strength they got themselves demolition jobs, knocking down a redundant barracks. For about three weeks they tottered into the Club each evening, a pallid grey colour from the combined effects of brick dust and physical exhaustion. Finally they gave up; it was too much for them. Carrots bummed around for a bit, but Stoker got himself a job grave-digging. He said it would get his muscles up just as well as the barracks, only more gradual.

His mates teased him about it a bit, saying that it was "a funny ole job an' all." Stoker replied, "It's a sight more normal, mate, than the line old Mike's took up." Mike, to everyone's astonishment, had become a police-cadet.

The first we all knew of it was when he appeared one evening wearing the uniform under his raincoat. He was obviously deeply self-conscious about it. He explained,

"Well, as you know, I've wanted for some time to get out of the rut, do something different. See all sorts and sizes of people and things. I reckon the Force will teach me a lot about life."

Apart from one or two derisive yells of, "Get back home, rozzer!" nobody made any really unfriendly remarks or gestures, which was gratifyingly restrained behaviour on the part of the kids, I thought, since at least half of them were sworn enemies of the Police.

Mike was helped no doubt by the fact that he had always been a popular and respected Club member.

He now took all the ribbing that came his way in good part. However we saw him but rarely, henceforth.

One evening he called in to see us at the same time as Chuck appeared, home on shore leave. Chuck had some pithy things to say to Mike about coppers. They stood talking in the Leader's office with Bertie and Clem chipping in the conversation from time to time, while Stoker used the Leader's typewriter to get off a letter to the local Bench, with whom he had recently had dealings. Spelling was not Stoker's strong point, so he kept appealing to Mike for help with a word.

"The cops is a loada fascists. I tell you mate, straight. You'll regret it," said Chuck to Mike.

"How d'you spell magistrate?"

"Know what they do at one nick I know of? They got three

C.I.D. blokes down there what take off their shoes an' kick you when you're fetched in; kick you all round the cell, they do. Fascists, they are."

"If they was real fascists they'd keep their shoes on," observed Clem.

"You ever bin kicked by them blokes, Chuck?" asked Bertie.

"No, I ain't, not person'ly, but I know two mates o' mine what has bin."

"The world is full of blokes who know blokes who've been beaten up by coppers," said Mike.

"You sayin' cops don't beat you up?"

"How d'you spell insurance?"

"Nobody denies that the police do just occasionally beat someone up but to make out that it's a routine thing is plain daft."

"Like to see old Mike beat Chuck 'ere up."

"Old Chuck's more likely to beat up old Mike."

"He better not; have the law on my side."

"Old Rory's the one to beat up geezers."

"Yeah mate, see old Rory go in fightin', blimey!"

"I ain't so bad when I get started," said Chuck, modestly. "How d'you spell excuse?"

And so on.

Stoker, having finished the letter, gave it, or rather showed it to me to see if it read well enough. This is what it said:

"To the Clark
  Magistrate Court
  In respect of
  Driving a motor-cycle
  without lisense (provinshal)
  without insurance
  driving 650 cc motor-bike on L-lisense my lisense took from me by Magistrates for two years my excuse for asking for lisense back is that I need my bike for driving to various youth centres to play in table-tennis teams, I cannot go without a bike, and for doing shopping for my parents saterday mornings saving fairs, my father cannot drive he has exsesive pains due to road axident that is my reason for wanting lisense back,
                    Yours Truly,
                      . . ."

Stoker was confident that this letter would work the trick. (It didn't).

Later that same evening, in the canteen, Carrots claimed that he could count a million in ten minutes. The other boys promptly told him to do it. He gabbled off the first hundred at top-speed, non-stop and then, scarlet in the face, had to pause to draw breath; whereupon Fred, who was timing him, said that he was disqualified.

This enraged Carrots, who declared that he hadn't had a fair chance. Things were becoming heated when fortunately Bertie interrupted to ask how long it would take to count a billion? Pete worked it out at 70,000 years. A second calculation brought it down to 700 years.

"Thass better," said Bertie.

"Yeah," said Carrots, "but who in hell's gonna last out 700 years to count it?"

Fred now worked it out in a different way and announced that eighty generations, counting non-stop from cradle to grave, would be necessary. There followed much hilarious comment on the notion of eighty babies, one after the other, starting to count at birth and continuing to count without pause until death released them at eighty.

"They wouldn't even 'ave no time to eat."

"Yeah, mate, they'd bloomin' die long before they reached eighty!"

"Keep them alive with injections," said Mike.

"What about sleep?"

"Train 'em to count in their sleep."

"But what about before they learned to talk, how they gonna count then?"

"Say goo-goo-goo."

Bertie again interrupted. This time he wanted to know what a generation was?

Finally Fred worked the whole thing out all over again and made the answer sixty million days; whereupon everyone agreed that "counting a billion just ain't bloomin' possible mate."

Mike looked in at the Club on one or two more occasions. In due course he finished his train'ng and became a fully-fledged P.C., after which his old haunts saw him no more.

We were now busy getting ready for another Christmas Fair.

The Mod girls flung themselves enthusiastically into making cards, calendars, match-box holders, cushions, soft-toys, cake decorations, table-mats and lamp-shades. The Rock girls dressed dolls and made baby-clothes. Mrs Z. and I decided to run a Christmas decoration stall. We turned up at the Club with armfuls of dried plant material; acorns, twigs, teasels, bits of bark and driftwood, pine-cones, silver and gold paint, glitter, glue, glass baubles. When we began to silver and glitter our dried material the Rock boys gathered round, watching breathlessly. Finally Gavin approached me closely and murmured, "Mrs B., can't I stick on some of them twinklers?"

In this way making Constance Spry-style Christmas decorations became an activity for our young male Rocks.

The Mod boys, on the other hand, enjoyed making painted wooden toys and lamp-stands.

The day of the Fair arrived; we had hired a hall this year near the town centre and in this way attracted many more people than we had the previous year. A number of local Youth Service people turned up and the Mayor also looked in, which was encouraging. All the stalls did well, especially the bottle-stall, the tombola and the White Elephant stall, while Bonny and Midge did a roaring trade in teas.

The way in which the Club members played an active part was really heartening. Pete, chain-smoking, ran a bran-tub for the tinies in the manner of a benign grand-father, Clem and Fred supervised the raffles, the first prize of the main raffle being a spectacular aurora borealis sweater knitted by poor dear Mr N., now on the last lap of life's strange journey, Gavin helped with the tombola, Mike served teas. All the girls made themselves helpful and delightful. Indeed it was downright touching to see all the members working so hard for the Club.

At the close of the afternoon Midge appeared wheeling a small trolley on which slopped perilously balanced cups of tea. He trundled the trolley up to Mrs Z. and myself, now dismantling our stall. "Ladies, the cup what cheers; I've fetched 'em special for you."

When our takings were all in we found that we had made over seventy pounds, which was marvellous. A staggering improvement on the previous year's pathetic effort.

It would have seemed from this that we had a bright and

prosperous New Year ahead. In actual fact the worst crisis of our history lay just round the corner. It was the winter of the Great Cold. Our Club was bad enough in an ordinary winter. We did not need the worst winter of the century to give us the impression that we were in the Arctic.

We were having sleety rain before Christmas; the roof was, as usual, leaking and the usual polite letter was sent to the local Authority. The Authority looked into the matter not only of the roof, but also of the lavatories, which were pretty disgraceful. We received a letter saying that repairs to roof and lavatories were estimated at a total cost of £900 and that this work was the responsibility of our landlord.

The Youth Officer then contacted the landlord on the Club's behalf. The landlord replied that he hadn't got £90, let alone £900.

We were still in the middle of this discussion when temperatures dropped, pipes froze, drains blocked, electricity and gas supplies were drastically cut, and all became chaos.

All youth-clubs suffered in terms of membership that winter. Few persons, young or old, wished to venture out in the evenings. Membership of our tomb-cold, desperately uncomfortable Club slumped to fifteen, and stayed there.

The fifteen members who continued to come to the Club were Gavin, Pete (now returned to the fold), Don, Fred, Clem, Bertie, Ian, Red (who came in late every evening, after he had seen his new girl-friend home), Carrots and Stoker, a small new member, Larry, and two sixteen-year-old new weight-training members, Mark and Grant. Only two girls came down; Dee and Morag. Dee because she was interested in Mark and Morag because she was interested in Ian.

All these boys, with the exception of Larry, were keen weight-trainers who would have gone anywhere, at any time, to pursue this activity. Larry loved the vaulting-horse and came down to the Club to indulge himself with that.

I had a vivid recollection of the first evening that I had encountered him. Very small, not yet fifteen, he had come into the canteen and had ordered and consumed five bags of Hamburger-flavoured potato-crisps washed down by five bottles of appleade.

I had said, "You're going it tonight."

"Gotta two quid pay-packet in my pocket, mate."

"Really? That's good. How d'you earn that?"

"Shifting boxes in the market. Do it every Sat'day. Another appleade, please."

He had drunk it direct from the bottle in one long, effortless swig. Then, putting the emptied bottle down on the canteen, he had wiped his mouth round with the back of a very grubby hand, had swung himself down off the bar stool and had said, casually, "Well s'long. Time for a go on the vaulting-horse." And off he had trotted for half-an-hour's very zesty P.T. After which he had returned for a night-cap of two cokes and two choc-bars.

Larry, in spite of the Great Cold, was still going strong: still patronizing the canteen lavishly on the proceeds of his pay-packets and vaulting afterwards with no sign of dyspepsia.

One advantage of such a small membership was that the atmosphere became very intimate and friendly. Barriers between adults and members thawed as the atmosphere outside steadily froze. We discussed, with increasing frankness, what was wrong with the Club. Why it went by such fits and starts; now bombing along happily, now running almost to a stand-still. Why it never, really, got off the ground for more than a short period at a time.

"At the present time it's understandable, like, that we got hardly nobody down here," said Fred. "But lookin' back right to the start, we've never really got going except in fits an' starts, have we? Get a good crowd together here, an' then they leave; get another crowd, then they leave."

" 'Course we've had bad luck with Leaders," said Clem.

"Yeah, but other clubs change Leaders, without having all the bleedin' ups an' downs we have."

"I know the weather's perishin' awful an' that," said Stoker, "but this place is almost dead. Other clubs is emptyish like, but not as dead as this place is."

"Thirteen blokes an' two bloomin' birds," said Ginger.

"Yeah, trouble with this joint is there's no birds no more," said Bertie.

"And to get birds you gotta have blokes," said Carrots. "Older blokes. Birds like older blokes. But the older blokes won't join if we ain't got no nice l'il birds. So whatsa score? Like what come first, the chicken or the sodding egg."

"Trouble is," said Ian, "you just can't ask a bird to this hole.

Straight, Mrs B., you can't ask a decent bird to come to a place with toilets like we got here. It's embarrassing for the bird and embarrassing for us."

"Yeah," said Carrots. "Stoker an' me met some real nice birds the other night at a party we went to; we'da liked to ask 'em along here, but you can't ask anyone along here to this Club the state it's all go t in. Straight you can't, Mrs B."

Bertie chipped in, "Mate, I dursn't ask any of my lot along here; itsa bleedin' shambles."

"Sorright for us lot, you see," added Clem. "It's our Club an' we're used to it like this. We meet each other here and get the weight-trainin' like and it's our Club, see? But you get a bloke what's used to one of those posh new clubs costin' thousands and he'd have a fit, see this place. And a decent bird, why, one look and a decent bird'd pass out."

"If she had time to, afore she froze to death," said Stoker.

"I know it was intended just as a club for a rough lot when it was opened," said Fred, "but it's really coming apart at the seams an' all now, innit?"

I went home that night in a very thoughtful mood.

A couple of nights later I again went to the Club. The Leader was there on duty single-handed.

A slight thaw had set in and the lugubrious sound of dripping water was to be heard in all directions.

Most of the boys were weight-training in the big hall. Dee was seated in the canteen, knitting a scarf. She wore an overcoat and fur-lined boots.

The Leader was standing by the sink trying to unscrew the cap from the waste-pipe. The pipe had been blocked for days.

In the lounge there was a fight going on, to judge by the noise.

"Evening, Mary. I thought I'd take advantage of the thaw to try to get this ruddy sink unblocked, but I can't get this damn cap unscrewed and some young bounder has pinched the footprints from the tool cupboard and . . . "

A deafening crash came from the lounge.

"It's Mark an' Grant having a go at Gavin and Larry," said Dee, calmly.

"They'll smash this place up worse than it already is while I'm wrestling with this wretched sink," said the Leader. "I shouldn't have to be doing this, you know; I'm a Leader, not a plumber. One's up against these premises and the problems they create all the time, Madam Chairman. They make it impossible for me to get down to my real job of work."

The sounds of fighting in the lounge swelled to crescendo and the Leader raced in there to investigate. Dee rose and moved away in the direction of the lavatories. I suspected that Mark and Gavin were fighting over her.

I stood in the shabby, shoddy, draughty, achingly cold canteen and stared at the sink full of repulsive water into which tea-leaves and coffee-dregs had been emptied until it looked like a peat-bog pool. I looked at the puddle on the floor beneath the leak in the canteen roof. I looked at the mildewy partition wall between the boys' urinals and the canteen.

The boys who had been fighting in the lounge now spilled into the canteen guffawing and swearing, the Leader after them all retribution. At that moment we heard Dee's voice shrieking from the girls' lavatories, "Guv'nor! Guv'nor! I can't get out!"

"What on earth?" I said.

"There aren't any door-handles in there, all ripped off," said the Leader. And he dived in the direction of the squealing Dee, returning a moment or two later with her, red-faced and giggling, in tow.

"All those handles were ripped off a fortnight ago. I never discovered who did it. I've asked the Youth Office to get them replaced, but nothing's happened yet. So if a girl shuts herself in the toilet she gets locked in," said the Leader. He recommenced fiddling with the sink. Dee turned on the juke-box and started to twist. Gavin, Pete, Mark and Grant started playing Monopoly. Leather jacketed and bescarved for warmth the four boys sat at a small battered table hard against the mildewed partition wall and traded earnestly for Mayfair hotels and City office-blocks. I said to the Leader, "We're simply wasting our time and energy trying to make a decomposed corpse viable, d'you know that?"

He looked up at me from where he crouched by the sink.

"This place," I said, "is an insult to all the kids who join the Club and all the adults who work here."

"You can say that again, Madam Chairman," he said.

"Come on, we'll make a complete tour of the premises here and now and get precisely everything down on paper. Strike while the iron's hot."

Without more ado we embarked on a hard-eyed tour of inspection. I wrote down all the findings as we went.

The canteen roof leaked. The lounge roof leaked over the corner where the darts-board was. The sky-lights were letting water, and there was a hole in the ceiling where the old stove-pipe had formerly been; the water dripping through this hole had saturated the sofa standing below. The builder had had this in hand for a long time. We were tired of writing letters about it.

We looked at the lavatories. Apart from being deathly cold they were saturated with damp. The boys' urinal reeked from stopped drains; the tank above leaked brown trails of slime over the walls. It was this leaking tank which affected the canteen wall.

An old sink had been placed, as a wash-basin, on the rusty stand of a defunct treadle-sewing machine. In this place the boys were supposed to change and rub down after weight-training, P.T. and so on.

The girls' lavatories were slightly better, but not much so.

We were, of course, still involved in argument about these lavatories, the local Authority claiming that the landlord was responsible and the landlord explaining that he had no money to repair them.

The floor in the gym hall had suffered always from rising-damp and had always been slippery, but now our new gas-heating had aggravated the situation and the floor was really dangerous. One boy had slipped recently, hit his head as he fell and all but knocked himself out. Worse accidents might happen any time.

The girls' powder-room was damp-proof, but had no heating and was like a refrigerator.

The Leader's office was the one place in the building that was really snug; but it had no daylight, which was a distinct disadvantage.

Dry-rot assailed much of the woodwork; the whole place had a musty, fungoid smell to which, I must confess, we had all become inured.

After our tour of inspection the Leader and I returned to the canteen and I brewed us each a coffee. This we sipped in despondent silence. At last I said,

"I'm a lousy chairman. For nearly two years I've been in office and it's only now that I've looked at the place objectively and discovered that it's a steaming dump and a screaming disgrace. I should be shot."

"This freak weather has shown it up," said the Leader. "Until now patching and making-do has carried the place along, but now this weather has shown it up."

"Shown me up too," I said.

A glasspane went in the hall. The Leader ran out to investigate. I remained brooding over my instant coffee.

Yes, we had patched things up and scraped along, always hoping for the best. We had made light of the bad condition of the premises; had declared that the buildings which house a youth-club were of secondary importance. It was the spirit of the Club itself that counted.

I didn't believe this any more. The Club had arrived at a moment of truth. Its much vaunted spirit was bogged down in a miasma of decrepitude.

When the weight-trainers flocked into the canteen for their customary coffee and a chat I told them that either we would get new premises, or close for good.

"Nobody," I said, "is going to waste further valuable time and energy in this hopeless place. It's all mildew and dry-rot and if we stick around here much longer we shall find ourselves getting mildew and dry-rot too!"

"You're dead right," they all said.

"What'll you do?" asked Ian.

"First I'll send a letter to end all letters to the Education people, telling them what it's really like down here and what we all really think about it. I've sent letters enough in the past, god knows, but I've been too lady like. This one will be a real letter."

"Yeah, mate," said Bertie, "send 'em a stinker. A real rocket up the arse-'ole."

"I will," I said.

CHAPTER XIII

HARD TRUTH AGAIN

NEXT DAY I wrote a long letter to the Education Officer which, if it did not exactly fit Bertie's lurid stipulation, was of a definitely urgent and emphatic nature. It described the state of the premises in detail and ended, I remember,

"It is therefore with reluctance that the Management Committee is forced to face the fact that the condition of the premises virtually renders further development of the Club impossible. For this Club to have any future alternative accommodation must be found in a building of decent fabric. How can we flourish, so long as we stand on fungoid feet under a rotting roof?"

This letter was submitted to our Management Committee, who approved of it unanimously and unhesitatingly. It was then dispatched without delay.

I also had a long interview with the Youth Officer, who assured me that he would back the Club up with all the power within his means.

A week later, in arctic weather (the thaw had given way to a new freeze) the Divisional Education Officer and the Deputy Chief Youth Officer came to look at the Club. The Leader and I showed them round. The premises were so bitterly cold that every word we uttered turned into clouds of steam. I reiterated, with as much passionate fervour as I could muster in such a low temperature, my major theme, that if our Club was considered by the Education Authority to be a worthwhile project then we must be given new premises where we could function properly and really carry the project through, but if the Authority did not feel prepared to support us with decent premises then the Management Committee and the Leader had absolutely no intention of trying to carry on with a club that was simply a waste of time, energy and public money.

Dancing up and down animatedly and beating their hands in an endeavour to keep warm (we were talking in the Club lounge), the visitors assured me of their interest in and sympathy for the Club and their realization of the important role it played in the local youth community and vowed that something would be done.

And something was done, too. Within a month it had been arranged that our Club should, as soon as possible, be transferred to a shortly-to-be-opened Youth Centre in a neighbouring part of the town.

This Centre was to be housed in a specially converted school, which I was taken to see. The exterior was early Victorian Gothic, very pleasing to the eye, but the interior, when the conversion was completed, would be streamlined contemporary.

The news that we were going to have a smashing new Club some time within the next few months had a wonderful effect on the Club members.

The Youth Officer handed me a copy of the plans for the new Centre and these I took to the Club for the members to see. The plans were put up on the Leader's office wall and everyone who called at the Club was at once taken to look. "Them plans there is our new Club. Luscious, innit?"

Meantime temporary improvements were carried out at our present Club. The lavatories were spruced up; a new tank and a new hand-basin were installed. Emergency repairs were carried out on the roof (and paid for by the County) and grant-aid was applied for so that we might get new furniture and equipment, since our aim was now to build up our membership so that when we did move to the new premises we could take with us a flourishing membership of some eighty to a hundred young people as a healthy nucleus for the Centre. Furniture and equipment, purchased now, could be transferred to the new premises.

Membership did begin to creep up again bit by bit. With the return of slightly warmer weather our Mod members reappeared. Paid-up membership stood at sixty, with an average nightly attendance of thirty.

Among the members who returned to us was Rory. He was most enthusiastic about the proposed move of the Club to new premises; indeed he appeared to be enthusiastic about the whole field of youth-work and spoke of training to become a Leader! The Youth Officer encouraged him.

"After all, Mary, the right help at the right time may make all the difference to that lad; I can think of a time in my life when I might have gone very badly off the rails myself if it hadn't been I was given a helping hand. Applies to a lot of us, no doubt. And if young Rory really set about it he'd make an excellent Leader, for he'd know how to reach and talk to the tough ones; aye, he'd be good."

So Rory was entered for the basic leadership-training-course that our Youth Office ran for young people.

Then Rory disappeared.

After a week or so of wondering what had happened to him news reached us that he had been turned out of the house by his father, his behaviour at home having become insupportable. He had moved into digs not far from the Club.

There was news, too, that he had not attended the opening session of the leadership-training-course. We feared that he might well be heading for trouble again.

The leader sent a message to the boy asking him to call at the Club.

In due course Rory appeared. He explained that he had not attended the leadership-course opening session because he hadn't any decent clothes to wear. Also he needed a suit to get a good job available to him in a local office. He required someone to stand as guarantor for him on a first down-payment on a suit to be bought on the H.P. Since his parents refused to have anything to do with him he wanted the Leader to put his name to the guarantee. The Leader was unwilling to do this, but suggested that the matter might be put to the Management Committee, who might think of some way of helping Rory.

Rory departed and the Leader telephoned me. I agreed to approach the Management Committee on Rory's behalf.

One evening, when I was at home cooking family supper, there was a smart knock on the front-door. I opened it and found myself face-to-face with a perfectly obvious plainclothesman; drab rain-coat, brown shoes, neat unsmartish suit, porkpie sort of hat, courteous smile, penetrating gaze. I started trying to think, in a panicky way, what I could have done. I am, by and large, a law-abiding citizen, but that C.I.D. look always makes me feel C.R.O.

My visitor turned out to be an ex-copper now employed as accounts investigator for a large tailoring firm.

My poor husband, resting by the fireside after a hard day's work, suddenly found himself confronted by this stranger, who was saying pleasantly, "Good-evening, sir. I'm from Q . . . the tailors. I've just called round to check, if I may, on your friend Rory . . . "

"Rory . . . ? Never heard of him," said Mr B.

"Indeed sir? He has given your name as guarantor on an order for items of clothing amounting to fifty-six pounds odd, sir."

I intervened. "Rory is one of my boys at the Club."

"Good God, I might have known it!" shouted Mr B. "Haven't I always said that that damn youth-club of yours would land us in trouble . . . " And so forth.

I served cups of tea, since our visitor declined sherry. He explained that Rory had ordered a suede jacket, a pair of boots, a raincoat, a sports jacket and two shirts. He had paid £5 down and had signed an agreement to pay the rest at fifty shillings a month over the next two years.

He had tried first to give the Club Management Committee as a guarantor, then my name, but as a woman I was un-acceptable, so finally he had given my husband's name.

I furnished the investigator with as glowing an account of Rory as I could, not because my husband was prepared to guarantee the purchases, he wasn't, but simply because I didn't want the boy's name to be black with the tailor.

There was no calculated intention on Rory's part, I was certain, to defraud anyone; no doubt he had the best of inten-tions with regard to paying the money. He liked good clothes (so do I) and this had seemed a heaven-sent way in which to equip himself with a nice little wardrobe. Yes, I understood perfectly and I was sorry that Rory must be disappointed; nonetheless his order had to be cancelled.

I must confess I rather wondered how he would take this; he was not the sweetest customer in the world when crossed. But when I met him later and said, "Sorry about the clothes, Rory, but you know, it simply wouldn't go," he merely smiled lightly and replied, "Sorry too, Mrs B. At the time I thought it was orright."

After this we didn't see him for a while. Tales reached us of changes of digs and various adventures. Then we heard that he had been slashed in a fight.

So the long, freezing winter gave way to a tardy spring. Work on the new Club premises had been badly held up by the weather, but now the workmen moved in and there were real signs of building activity. The Youth Officer escorted me to the site on frequent visits of inspection; we teetered up and down planks stretched perilously across drainholes, inhaled grit, got more grit in our shoes, and on one occasion had a quantity of old plaster and fragments of brick shovelled over us through a window. We spoke enthusiastically together about how delightful the new Club was going to be.

"Och, they're getting on well with it, now, Mary."

"Indeed they are. It's terrific."

Back at the Club the usual summer activities commenced: swimming, adventure sessions, week-end camps on the Downs, by the coast. The Southend walk was fixed this year for mid-June and everyone began to talk in terms of training. Rory reappeared at the Club and assured the Leader that he would do the walk this year in record time.

He came into the canteen, greeted me amiably. His left eyebrow was badly split; I did not ask him how he had done it. He began telling me that he was living back home again and then, following some line of thought doubtless clear enough to him although obscure to me, he said, "Course, you know all this parta the town is built on ole water-cress beds?"

"Is it? I never knew that."

"Splains the damp, mate."

"Indeed it does."

"Scandal, really, Still in them days they didn't care. There's water oozin' all under here."

He began eating a hot-dog.

"I'm goin' up Box Hill, Sunday, with twenty-five pounds weighta sand in a rucksack; toughen meself for the Southend Walk. You comin'? Box Hill, nex' Sunday."

"I'm afraid not. In actual fact I'm going up to the Lake District in a day or two and on Sunday, with a bit of luck, I shall be on Scafell."

"I envy you," said Rory. There was real longing in his voice. "That'd suit me."

I thought that it would. Nature had not designed him for a twentieth-century bricks-and-mortar environment.

We chatted about his job, his family and so forth. The Leader came up and asked him about some records. It transpired that Rory had borrowed several recently from the Club and, in returning them, had failed to bring back the two newest. Rory seemed genuinely distressed about this; he kept raising his right hand above his head, as if automatically taking an oath, and exclaiming in his "truthful" voice (like all persons who have made frequent appearances in the dock he had a special voice for giving evidence, as it were, on his own behalf), "You know it wasn't intended, don't you guv? Know I didn't intend it."

The Leader said that of course he knew it wasn't intended, but they were two of the latest Hit-Parade discs and the other members wanted them back badly. Rory, oozing apologetic charm, went off on his bike to fetch the discs.

So the summer wore on. The Southend Walk never came off; Clem went on holiday, Fred was working flat-out for an exam, Bertie excused himself on the understandable grounds that "me feet give me bleedin' agony last year mate; 's not worth it." While Rory, after all his brave talk of training, disappeared; he had left home again.

We held a Parents' Evening; we now had seventy Club members and we issued individual invitations to all the parents, by post. Six parents came.

Members went off on holiday and sent us vividly coloured post-cards; the Costa Brava, Majorca, Isle of Wight, Copenhagen, Lugano, Land's End. Our weight-trainer sent us a postcard of his hotel at San Sebastian with his bedroom marked with an X. Dee and Mark went to Colwyn Bay together and sent us a postcard showing their hotel and *their* bedroom window marked with an X. The card said,

"Dear Everybody, having a smashing time. Wish you were all here (ha! ha!) Went up Snowdon yesterday; train. Sat on beach all today. Lots of sun and grub. Yours to a cinder. Dee and Mark."

Dee and Mark were sixteen.

Bonny stared thoughtfully at the card. "Summertime, and the living so easy," she said.

And then it was time to close the Club for the summer recess and for us all to take our holidays and go away and then it was time to come back again and reopen the Club and know that summer was over and winter on its way back.

We had hoped, of course, that the new autumn session would see us installed in the new Centre. The work on the project had been seriously delayed, however, by objections of people living near the proposed Centre. Understandably they didn't welcome a Youth Centre on their doorsteps. Nevertheless there have to be Youth Centres and I can only suggest to persons who do happen to land one in their near neighbourhood to make the best of a bad job, call on the Leader and offer friendship and support. If you can't beat 'em, join 'em.

So the autumn found us still in our old premises. The local objections to the Centre were finally overcome, but there could now be no possible prospect of our moving before Spring at the earliest.

Bonny C. was now obliged to leave us, for health reasons. Luckily we were able to get another woman assistant to replace her without too much delay. The newcomer was Anne Figgart; youthfully mature, attractive, with a wonderful warmth of personality which radiated from her. She obviously loved young people, and they loved her. In no time at all Mrs Figgart had become our dear one and only Figgy.

But, in spite of the stimulating and happy presence of Figgy and the knowledge that the new Centre was only just round the corner and moving there was now but a matter of patience, things were not going well with the Club. Membership figures slowly and steadily fell. New members joined, but they did not stay. Clearly something was radically amiss once more. But what was it this time?

The roof had been repatched and money had been spent generously on the sort of equipment and fittings that could be taken with us when we moved. So the Club, although still far from what was ideal for a youth-club, was physically much more attractive than it had been. One could no longer automatically blame the premises themselves for lack of success.

So what was it?

Gradually the comments and general behaviour of the members themselves provided a clue to the trouble. The Club had become overdisciplined.

When our Leader had come to us at first, a climb out of the chaos resulting from a long period of *laissez-faire* and leaderlessness had pleased the members; young people don't really enjoy a wholly permissive club. But this discipline thing is like a swing-boat; there is a very low moment, which is unpleasant, and a very high moment, equally unpleasant. The delightful moment is that instant of balance when one is poised between the two extremes.

So it was with our Club. Our Leader had certainly had a moment of real success, achieved in that period of balance between insufficient discipline and too much discipline. But we now had swung too far in the opposite direction of *laissez-faire* and were gripped in an atmosphere of excessive control.

All the symptoms were present. Membership and general morale declined. The Mods, the least rebellious of the members, fluctuated in their attendance, failing to turn up particularly on those occasions when they had undertaken to attend for some specific activity. They bickered amongst themselves when they were present.

The Rocks, always more openly rebellious, made their opinion of the Leader fairly obvious. One or two of them made no bones of telling me how they now felt about the way in which he was running the Club. Others revealed their resentment more obliquely; they damaged equipment, smashed the juke-box and so forth, although surreptitiously, so that nobody was actually ever caught. They broke rules "by mistake", tended not to hear orders, went quietly out of their way to displease. They were openly aggressive to one another and in a round-about manner to the Leader himself.

He came into the canteen one evening and told me jubilantly that he had visited the dentist and had been told that his teeth were in excellent condition; good for another forty years! "I shan't have to bother with dentures, Mary!" Laughing he went into the gym to spar with Carrots. Some twenty minutes later the poor Leader stumbled into the canteen, bleeding from the mouth and holding his jaw. "That damn boy has cracked two of my back teeth. Rot him, he's dislodged at least a couple of molars with a real block-buster."

"And they were to last another forty years!" I cried.

He grinned wryly. Carrots came into the canteen and began apologizing profusely, but I could not resist wondering if it had not been one of those interesting accidents that are done on purpose.

So the winter advanced and membership dwindled. The weight-training group alone flourished. Grant took part in a contest and became champion for the south-east area in the ten stone class.

Dee caused a sensation by dropping Mark abruptly and marrying Pete. We did not see her at the Club again. To date,

three years later, the marriage has been a success. There is one
child and Dee makes a very excellent little mother.

Figgy and I started cookery sessions again. They went very
well, though from the start the boys seemed more interested in
cookery than the girls were.

So things jogged on while the Leader, after a long talk with
the Youth Officer and me, tried a more relaxed approach
towards the members.

The Beatles were now all the rage, their *Twist and Shout*
deafened us nightly. All the girls were crazy over them,
especially a newcomer named Babette, a small, brittle, spark-
like red-head. She liked to have the Beatles on non-stop, full-
blast. At the same time she ogled Mark, unashamedly. "Come a
little closer now!" roared the Beatles. Babette wriggled in front
of Mark and laughed in his face. He came a little closer.

One evening Figgy was showing the girls how to make scotch-
eggs, while I served in the canteen. The cookery was hampered
by Babette. She didn't want to cook, so she had turned the juke-
box on at its loudest pitch and with two mates was twisting
dementedly, a couple of feet from the juke-box. Figgy and I
tried to carry on with the scotch-eggs and the canteen as if no
juke-box were deafening us, although our heads were zinging
and we couldn't hear ourselves speak. The important thing was
not to let dear little Babette see that she was in any way
annoying us. Her anti-social behaviour must fall flat.

Presently Bertie came into the canteen, stooped over the gas-
ring to light a cigarette and singed off one eyebrow and a lump
of fringe. Then Mrs Z. looked in to chat about colour-schemes
for the new Centre, but could not make herself heard above the
juke-box, so she ate a scotch-egg and went away. Then the
Youth Officer turned up and ate two scotch-eggs. He informed
us that Rory had just gone inside again; four months, Wandsworth.

Finally Babette deserted the juke-box for a ride on the pillion
of Mark's bike and peace descended. The Leader joined me in
the canteen for a coffee. He said,

"You've a rum lot of youngsters in this town, Mary. Can't
reach 'em, somehow."

"Cheer up," I said. "You reached them very well at one
point, and what you've managed once you'll manage again."

"I used to think that too, but not any more. They baffle me.

6*

I just can't reach 'em. You had what you called your moment of truth with the premises; well, this is my moment of truth with the members down here."

"You'll make it with them again, don't worry," I said.

But he believed otherwise and left us for a club in the West Country. Once more we were without a Leader.

PART FIVE

SUMMER VIOLENCE

"At that time I had a brother two years younger than myself, a very daring, proud-spirited lad . . . This child was then about fourteen, and I was two years older. One Sunday about two hours before nightfall . . . he fell out with a young man of twenty or so. They fought with swords, and so valorously did he close with his opponent that he dealt him a serious wound, and was for following the thing up. Among the crowd that stood about were many of the young man's kinsfolk, who seeing the affair go ill with him, took out their slings. One of the stones struck my poor young brother's head, and he fell suddenly to the ground, where he lay senseless as if dead . . . Running to him speedily, I took his sword and planted myself between him and the other threatening swords and the shower of stones. Nor did I leave him till [there] came up some valiant fighting men and saved me from the wild rage of the crowd . . . Then I carried my unconscious brother home, where with much difficulty he came to his senses . . . "

"It happened one day I was leaning up against [a] shop . . . While I stood there talking one of the family, their cousin . . . waited till there came by a beast of burden with a load of bricks; and when the beast was just opposite, shoved it on me with such force that I was much hurt. Turning suddenly and seeing that he was laughing, I dealt him such a blow with my fist on his temple that he fell in a dead faint. Then facing his cousin, I said, "That's what thieves and cowards of your sort get." They made as if to attack me . . . and I whose blood was boiling, put my hand on a little knife I had, and roared, "If one of you dares come out of the shop, the other can run for the priest: there will be nothing for the doctor to do!"

Benvenuto Cellini (1500 – 1571). Memoirs

CHAPTER XIV

YOUNG LIONS

THE MANAGEMENT COMMITTEE in consultation with the local Youth Committee decided to tide over the months before we moved to the Centre by employing part-time Leaders, rather than to try to find a new full-time Leader at this stage. Obviously the full-time Leader for the new Centre would have to be very carefully selected. We would want somebody of the highest calibre possible.

We had Figgy at the Club three nights a week and to help her we now got a qualified assistant male Leader, named Gus, for two nights and a young Irishman, Driscoll O'C., as a voluntary assistant two nights of the week. Driscoll thought that he might like to make youth-work his career, but wished to find out something about it before he committed himself. Poor young man, he was certainly to find out!

The Club members, naturally interested in our choice of new full-time Leader, had several earnest conversations with me on the subject. Stoker said,

"O.K., so you need someone who can keep us lot in order. Fair enough. But it can be carried too far. You gotta strike the happy medium, Mrs B."

"Easier said than done," I sighed.

"Yeah, I know that; not saying it's easy to find the right bloke for this job. 'Ere, tell you what, next time let us lot choose the Leader. We know what's needed. Let us pick him for you."

"Yes, let us lot pick him," chorused the other boys.

"We got a lotta very sensible ideas about youth-clubs now," said Stoker. "Gettin' experienced like."

The Youth Office was, in fact, most interested at this time in the views of young people themselves upon the subject of clubs. It was becoming clear that clubs, as clubs, were no longer so popular as they had been. The problem was what to put in their place? Youth coffee-bars, once a very popular idea with progressive youth-workers, were now pretty well as old hat as straightforward clubs.

Figgy and I held, and taped, some very interesting informal discussions with the senior members on this subject.

Almost all the members who took part in these discussions thought that clubs should be "more social, like, with more facilities for older members." There was a particularly long and lively discussion about whether youth-clubs should be licensed, but general opinion was against this. Nearly all the boys thought that the age-limit should be extended; the girls did not agree, they thought "you're grown out of youth-clubs by the time you're twenty."

One boy wanted a club where "Elderly members can come and discuss their marriages together." By elderly, it transpired that he was thinking of people of "round about twenty-eight."

One fact emerged very clearly; many of the young people felt the need of places where they might talk over personal problems and receive advice. In short, youth advisory bureaus.

Our Club was now picking up again, in spite of the prevalent view that clubs were out of date. The answer was that the sort of members we catered for needed clubs more than any other section of the youth community, and experience was at last teaching us to try to give the members the kind of club that they wanted, rather than the kind of club we adults thought that they should have.

The Club atmosphere had now become considerably more relaxed, without, however, becoming actually permissive. Figgy was trying hard to achieve a balance and she would probably have succeeded without too much trouble if the summer (1964) had not exploded into one of teenage violence.

In May there occurred the first of the South Coast so-called Mod-Rocker Riots. It so happened that an acquaintance of mine, a very experienced social worker, most competent to judge, was present at this first, alleged riot, and she assured me afterwards that the affair was in reality no more than an incident. It is the view of many professional youth-workers that irresponsible Press publicity and hysterical public reaction ballooned the thing out of all proportion. After the first "riot" newspaper readers couldn't wait for more; where would the Mods and Rocks strike next?

So the thing built up. Without the publicity the sea-front scenes would in all likelihood have quickly fizzled out.

On the evening following the Whit Monday of the initial

"riot" only one member at our Club showed any interest in the incident and that was Bertie. He had spent the first part of the evening in our canteen quietly drinking coffee, but at 9.45 he rose, put on his skid-lid and leather gloves, and enquired, "Who's turnin' out for a fight?"

"Fight who?" asked Mark.

"Outside the coffee-bar. They gonna beat up the Mods."

There was a brief silence while Bertie surveyed his cronies amiably. "None o' you lot comin'? Be great. Real kicks."

He turned and grasped the door-handle to let himself out. Mark, Grant, Skid and one or two others shifted in their seats as if half a mind to follow. Bertie said again, "Real kicks." I leaned over the canteen-counter and shouted at him, "Bertie, don't be a bloody fool!"

Thoroughly startled, and not a little indignant, he turned and treated me to one of his famous, slew-headed scowls. "Wha?"

"If you want to beat up a Mod, beat up Don here." Don was our beefiest Mod. He was also immeasurably placid and friendly. He was, at this moment, seated on a bar-stool tranquilly eating a hot-dog. He looked at me with as much astonishment as poor Bertie was showing.

"Beat that geezer up?" said Bertie at last. "Whaffor?"

"If you've no reason to beat up some Mod you *do* know, why in hell d'you want to get out there and beat up a total stranger? What on earth's the point in that?"

Bertie stood scowling harder than ever. Don began grinning broadly.

"What crazy nonsense," I continued, swabbing down the canteen counter as I talked, "to beat up people you've never set eyes on before in your life, for no reason at all."

Bertie shook his head, indicating pity for me. Then very slowly he sat down, took off his gloves and lit a cigarette.

We now suffered another of those virtual over-night changes in membership.

Fred left the Club. He had been with us ever since we had opened in 1959 and had become very much a part of us. But he was now growing up fast; in point of fact he had outgrown us. Sad as it is, everyone outgrows their adolescent haunts. Fred was no exception.

Unfortunately, when he left us most of our Mods left too. He had been, as it were, their private leader.

The departure of Sally, Sue, Morag, Ian, Don and the rest deprived us, at one fell stroke, of a sizable slice of membership; we found ourselves left with a much smaller and totally different kind of Club. The submerged Rock element, no longer sub-merged, took over.

Our street frontage throbbed with big motor-bikes. Leather jackets intricately patterned with brass studs became the In-gear, together with buccaneer-long hair for the boys. The Rock birds appeared in black tights, high boots and chunky dark sweaters. They reminded me of plump, yet lithe, little cats. They were a very different sight from Sue, Sally and Morag in their Liberty prints and ankle-length tweed skirts.

Talking of long hair on boys, I discovered that one could often gauge the state of a boy's relationship with his parents, especially with his father, from the length of his hair. The longer the hair, the worse the relationship.

One of our Club boys was a particularly good example. When he joined he was on poor terms with his father. Hair was long and scruffy. Terms improved a little, hair was trimmed slightly. Boy made friends with a youth of whom father strongly disap-proved; hair grew long again and sideburns were cultivated. Friendship with undesirable crony ripened; hair grew longer and longer, sideburns turned into Blackbeard the Pirate trimmings. Then friendship with undesirable started to wither. Sideburns diminished accordingly. Friendship more or less ceased; got rid of sideburns and had hair slightly trimmed. Relationship with father improved; hair was thinned, finally an inch was cut right off. Lapse of time during which hair was not cut any shorter, but became very clean and shiny; shampoo was obviously being showered upon it, regardless of cost. Boy had got himself a girl-friend. Father didn't think much of girl-friend though. Hair grew a good inch, but remained beautifully clean. Finally father thawed towards girl-friend; off came some more hair. Father gave son a generous down-payment on smashing new bike; boy appeared with conventional short-back-and-sides.

With the advance of summer there was a wave of general teen-age violence. Inter-club fights became uncomfortably prevalent; gang-warfare spread from district to district. The sensational Mod-Rock publicity had borne fruit, as youth-workers had feared it might. Not that Mod-Rock animosity was in fact the major feature of the summer's fighting, which was in point of fact based on the feuds and skirmishing habits which always lie dormant (and always have) beneath a certain section of the youth community. But the Mod-Rock publicity had excited this undercurrent of chronic violence; the smouldering embers fanned into lively flames.

We live in a violent age and the young of today are very much more violently inclined than were their grand-parents and great-grandparents. The Edwardian and Victorian eras were, in retrospect, enormously civilized, peaceful, smug periods, strong in bourgois moral values and virtues. All this exploded in 1914. There are still people alive who can remember the pre-1914 era and whose moral and social values are strongly grounded in that era. Many of today's accepted values linger from that relatively peaceful and Christian era. But today does not belong to that era and for anyone born after 1918 that era has a dream-like, unreal atmosphere, like a miracle plum-cake that appeared from heaven, was tasted by some lucky people, and then withdrawn, leaving behind it a great smacking of lips and nostalgic sighing.

I was born after that plum-cake went fut. True, I was brought up on recipes founded upon it, and have listened politely to the reminiscences and philosophies of persons reared on the genuine article, but the time has come to face the fact that that plum-cake has absolutely gone, and won't come back, and that the only people who now have the slightest belief in that plum-cake are those who in their old age are suffering from indigestion and can taste the cake, as it were, repeating itself. Leaving these persons to regurgitate, the rest of us must move on in search of a new recipe.

One feels, in this violent and insecure world of today, that the distant part is often more easily understandable than the yesterday of the plum-cake era. I feel utterly estranged, for instance, from the young Max Beerbohm, elegant in his frock-coat and top-hat, making calls at equally elegant London houses and leaving his cards. I feel much closer to the young Benvenuto Cellini, getting involved in a street punch-up and pulling out a knife. Max Beerbohm lived in this century and at the end of the last; Cellini was street-brawling four hundred odd years ago. But although I have never in my life seen a young man paying social calls garbed in a frock-coat and a top-hat, I have seen a punch-up, and watched a boy pull out a knife. I know what a street fight sounds like, and looks like and smells like; I know of hansom cabs only by hearsay.

And if I, who am middle-aged, feel like this, is it any wonder that the really young are totally out of touch and sympathy with that lost world of yesterday which so many older people will insist upon speaking of as a sort of heritage?

The truly young today have nothing of that plum-cake in their veins. What they have is derived from further back.

But to return to the fighting that summer. As I have explained, we had a well-established fighting element in our town and the juveniles of this fighting element had, from the first, formed a nucleus of our tougher Club members. We enjoyed (perhaps that is not quite the right word) the constant patronage of the offspring of two of the best-known fighting families in the district. These youngsters joined the Club in relays; the families were remarkably prolific and directly one batch of battling members reached the Club age-limit a fresh contingent marched in further down the age-scale.

Despite this we had never, as yet, become involved in definite gang-warfare.

Our troubles, this summer, began with an incident of vandalism. Mark and Stoker, complaining one evening that they had nothing to do, commenced to slash chairs, kick in a door, break windows and so on. Driscoll O'C. began shouting discipline in a very loud voice, but lacked the know-how to restore order (admittedly it is very difficult to restore order in such circumstances). In his panic he called upon the weight-trainers to make Mark and his mates behave. Out came the weight-trainers, not indisposed to enjoy a punch-up since authority had given them the green-light. Not surprisingly a first-rate battle was soon raging. It ended quite abruptly, however, because of an unlooked for development.

One of our main fighting families rejoiced in the name of Patchey (the other lot were Chooseys). The Patcheys were cousins of the redoubtable Rory. The Patcheys were a very closely-knit clan; mix it with just one Patchey, in an empty street, and before you knew where you were you miraculously had the whole family on top of you. During the course of this Club fight Titch Patchey, the smallest boy, was in his opinion foully held down and punched. He began to holler blue murder. His oldest sister, Camilla, seeing what had happened, at once dispatched the smallest girl, Estella, round home (only a street distant) to fetch cousin Rory, just back from Wandsworth. Off scuttled Estella while Camilla pitched herself, tooth and nail, upon Titch's assailants. Winston and Humph, the middle Patchey boys, had of course been in the thick of the scrimmage since the word go.

In answer to the family S.O.S. there quickly appeared Rory, fresh from the flowery, and breathing fire and slaughter.

Upon the appearance of Rory all the other contestants melted away. Such was his reputation.

He was in a very ugly mood and stood there demanding to know which dirty bastard had been punching up young Titch?

Figgy (who had never met Rory but had heard a lot about him) went quietly up to him and asked him if he were a Club member. He replied that he wasn't, whereat she tapped him firmly on the shoulder and said, "Then out!" Rory was both highly annoyed and totally nonplussed; before he knew where he was, the astounding little woman had him in the street. He protested verbally (most unusual for him, he generally protested with his fists) and all the cousins came out on to the pavement and protested likewise, on his behalf. But Figgy stood firm and at last the clan marched home. Back there Rory held an enquiry into the fight and decided that Titch had had no legitimate grounds for complaint, he had been hurt by a straight-forward punch in a perfectly straight fight. So Rory at once returned to the Club, apologized to Figgy for his behaviour and said that he would be happy to offer his services to the Club in any way they might be desired or required.

He was therefore installed as a senior helper.

"Round and round we go," said the Youth Officer.

He himself dealt with Mark, Skid and Stoker, who had started the trouble in the first place. The Youth Officer was a former army P.T. instructor and, since these three trouble-makers had allegedly taken to destruction because they "had nothing to do", he declared that they should henceforth damn well have something to do; a series of P.T. sessions with him that would, he swore, kill them. "Even if it means, Mary, that I finish by killing myself. If it's my last act I'll give those three young villains something they won't forget in a hurry."

Mark, Skid and Stoker were accordingly given a vintage

evening. They emerged from it with flying-colours. The Youth
Officer telephoned me to say that they were three remarkable
boys, full of promise, a pleasure to train, first-rate material and
so forth. Moreover they had actually asked for regular P.T.
sessions with him and he had promised that he would give them
to them.

As for the boys, they privately told me, "You should see 'im,
like he was made of indiarubber or something. To look at that
geezer you'd think he was pretty well past it, wouldn't you?
But mate, he's a flippin' marvel."

The Youth Officer was in the good books of the members.
Not everyone was so lucky.

The following Tuesday I went to the Club to partner Driscoll,
who was on duty alone there, since Figgy was on holiday and it
was our other part-time Leader's night off. Directly I arrived at
the Club I smelt the intangible, but unmistakable, smell of
trouble. There was another smell too as I advanced into the
canteen; the acrid odour of stink-bombs. Driscoll stood distraught in the centre of the canteen, wailing at me, "Oh, it's
thim Patchey lads, they should be turned out! They're an
unholy mob, the lot of them, an unholy mob and in a terrible
state this evenin', wild as young lions, but oh 'tis the Patchey
boys that's the worst!"

Thus he stood keening.

There was a tremendous din going on and even as he spoke a
fresh batch of stink-bombs were set off; clouds of sulphurous
smoke eddied round us; through it I perceived the boys, pacing
and wheeling, like lithe and threatening young carnivores,
their prey most undoubtedly the wretched Driscoll. "You
should get rid of those Patchey boys! They're behind all this
trouble!" "Try to take no notice," I said, stifling the cough
which the smoke had brought on, "take no notice, it's early in
the evening yet and if we take no notice the chances are it'll all
die down. They're only doing it to see how you react."

Buzz, a boy very keen on cooking, came into the canteen
carrying a bottle of milk. "This milk's turned, Mrs B. Can I
use it to make a batch of scones?" "Anything you like, Buzz,
anything you like," I said. "What's the trouble down here
tonight, anyway?"

"Dunno," said Buzz vaguely. "Ole Winnie's a bit mad over
something I guess."

Winnie was Winston Patchey.

Something went with a crash in the rear hall. Driscoll ran to look. I put on the kettle to make coffee. Buzz started scouring the washing-up bowl to use as a mixing bowl. After he had cleaned the bowl he surveyed his hands; since he was a motor-bike enthusiast they were black with oily muck. "Maybe I oughter wash me mitts too." "Wouldn't be a bad idea," I said. So he gave his hands a good going over with Vim.

Something else went crash, followed by yells of laughter.

Buzz set about the scone mixture in a most competent manner. He soon had a nice-looking batch of scones in the oven and the lower set of canteen-shutters up to exclude draughts. "Can't have draughts when you're baking."

Meanwhile little Titch Patchey let off a lot more stink-bombs. Other kids burned up the ping-pong net, burned several holes in items of furniture and smashed a door panel. Driscoll dashed from one spot of sabotage to the next, but always arrived just too late to catch anybody in the act.

Although there could be no doubt that Titch and Winston were the prime instigators it was clear that the rest of the members were cheerfully in cahoots with them. They were all out to give Driscoll one hell of an awful evening.

He ran round and round in dreadful agitation. I repeated, "Best take no notice. We can't stop them by force, so leave 'em to simmer in their own juice a bit and pretend it doesn't worry you. Let it all fall flat. If it gets too bad we'll shut the Club early. Meantime let it all fall flat."

But he continued to fuss, wail and protest.

Skid got locked in a lavatory. He was apparently stooping down examining the lock as a preliminary step towards attempted self-release when some other boy kicked the door open, catching Skid full in the face. He came staggering into the canteen with the blood trickling down his cheek; he looked muzzy and very pale. For the first time that evening I began to feel rather scared. Buzz was now meticulously testing the scones to see if they were properly cooked. I applied cold compresses to Skid's contused forehead; the boy, dazed and in considerable pain, leaned groggily against me while I pressed the compress against his blood-oozing skin.

"You think they're done, Mrs B.? They seem orright to me," said Buzz, indicating the scones.

Skid meantime kept saying feebly, "I'm orright Mrs B. It's nothing really."

Rory suddenly appeared, dressed dead posh as Buzz remarked. He was done up like the complete puppy-dog's dinner. I said, "Oh Rory, I'm glad you've come. It's a shambles here tonight." He said, "Can't stay I'm afraid, Mrs B. Got a date with my bird." And off he went.

"Some senior helper," I said angrily. But pretty obviously Rory, besides having a date, also knew that his young cousins were on the rampage and he had no desire to remain at the Club and find himself obliged to hand out disciplinary methods against them.

After Rory had stalked out another stick of stink-bombs was released, the leg of a chair was burned and the lights were fused in the lounge.

Meanwhile Buzz, totally unperturbed by all this, took twelve luscious-looking scones from the oven, keeping the thirteenth and largest for himself. The twelve were put out for sale, each on a separate plate with a dab of butter, for a penny per portion; much too cheap, but I was too hard-pressed for discussions on domestic economy, so the scones-and-butter sold as real bargains. They were so delicious that would-be purchasers were swarming and scrapping all over the canteen-counter for them. It was bedlam.

"Like a taster, Mrs B.?" shouted Buzz. He gave me a bit of his scone; the boy could certainly bake. But when I asked him what ingredients he had used, and in what proportion, he replied vaguely, "Same as if you was mixing cement."

Skid sat down on a chair, I gave him coffee and Buzz saw that he got a scone-and-butter, for free. A football thwacked, full force, into the canteen-shutters behind us. It reminded me of the Blitz.

The Youth Officer looked in, on his evening rounds. His appearance caused a temporary lull in the terror-campaign. He and I had a muttered conversation. "Driscoll O'C. will have to go," I said. "He's more trouble than he's worth. He makes them behave worse, with all his wailing." "Close the Club now, Mary, and keep it closed for the rest of the week. Things are getting very out of hand." "No," I said, "that's too much like defeat."

He could not stay, so we agreed to meet and confer on the morrow. Immediately he had walked out of the Club the youngest Choosey fixed another stink-bomb to the office-door; it not only made a gruesome smell but also burned a round, black hole in the door-panel.

I walked up close to the door and stood watching the smoke trickling from the hole. The child watched me watching. At last he said, with a grin, "Dontcher mind?"

"Why should I? It's your funeral, not mine. This is your Club, not my Club." The smoke curled up. "The cost of all this damage will go on the subs," I said, raising my voice. "Everyone will pay more. Raise the money for repairs that way. Then you can get a work-party together and repair all the damage."

"Oh yeah?" said Titch. "What if we don't?"

"Then the Club will stay closed until you do."

"What, none of us come in? Even us lot that ain't done no damage?" asked another voice.

"Closed to the whole lot of you. And you all get extra on the subs, too."

All the other kids began to bellow and howl and say no, they'd done nothing, it wasn't fair that they should all suffer for what just a few had done.

I said, "This Club is the club of you all and if none of you has the guts or the gumption to put a stop to this silly behaviour on the part of a foolish few then it's just too bad, you'll all have to suffer."

I was thinking that I was about to recapture some kind of authority over them when fresh wails were heard from Driscoll. He appeared wringing his hands and gasping something about murder. This ruined the moment. The kids burst into shrieks of derisive laughter. "You come and look at this, Madam Chairman!" cried Driscoll. I followed Driscoll into the little committee room, which was plunged in darkness, apart from a shaft of light falling through the doorway. Dimly I made out young Larry lying lashed to the table, trussed with electric-light flex which had been wrenched, complete with bulb and shade, from the ceiling.

I went to the phone and put through an urgent call to the Vice-Chairman. He came round right away.

On seeing him Winston and Humph Patchey untied Larry, who was fortunately not hurt and indeed insisted that it was quite all right; just done for kicks.

More stink-bombs were let off while the Vice-Chairman and

I held a council of war in the canteen. "Ignore the things, Mary," gasped the Vice-Chairman. "Pretend they don't bother us. Awful frost."

"What a smell, och what a smell!" cried Driscoll. The Vice-Chairman said, "Been to Wimbledon this year, Mary?"

"No. Have you?"

"Yes. I was there yesterday. Saw a splendid match."

"Coo, don't these things half smell!" said Estella Patchey. "Don't it make your eyes water, Mrs B.?"

"No. Does it yours?"

"Yes. It do. Somethink awful. Makes me cough, too."

Driscoll lamented like Anna Livia Plurabelle. "What a night! What a night! Never in me worst hours! You'll have to get rid of them Patchey boys!"

"Stick it out till closing-time," said the Vice-Chairman. "Never let the little devils get the best of the day."

Closing time was now only thirty minutes away and somehow we hung on. Humph, Winston and their set drove off on their bikes shortly after the Vice-Chairman turned up, but Titch remained behind to whip the little boys into a final frenzy of stinks and pranks. There was a plot afoot amongst them in the last few moments; they kept trying to steal back into the Club, possibly to plant a bomb which would explode and set the premises on fire after we had all left (I had reached the stage where I would have put nothing past them). But now I was, belatedly, getting into my stride too. I had got the strength of these younger ones. Every time they stole back, in ones and twos, I waylaid them in the lobby with motherly enquiries as to whether they had forgotten their gloves, jackets. They glared at me, muttered, shuffled their feet. I smiled the sweetest smiles, positively cooed. "What can I do for you, my little dears?" Disgusted, they ultimately dispersed.

The Vice-Chairman and I locked up and saw Driscoll safely away; we had rather feared that he might be ambushed. But the street was quiet and empty and the only signs of defiance were the obscenities scrawled on the roof of the Vice-Chairman's Mini.

"Ah well, it was due for a wash," said he, philosophically. "What's the betting that poor young chap will decide against taking up youth-work?"

But I couldn't answer. I was at last able to cough. I leaned against the Mini and coughed until I thought my head would split.

CHAPTER XV

L'IL OLE FIG

THE FOLLOWING EVENING the Youth Officer and I each had a talk with the Patchey boys. They were told precisely what we thought of them; they took it very well and agreed to form a working-party to make good the damage that they had done.

Winston, their spokesman, gave an explanation for their behaviour. They had had it in for Driscoll O'C., he said, because they hadn't liked the way in which he had recently spoken to Titch Patchey whom he had suspected of trying to knock-off a bottle of pop. So Winston had got up a petition asking Mr O'C. to resign. This had been handed to Mr O'C. shortly before I had arrived at the Club, the previous evening, the evening of the trouble. Driscoll had not mentioned this petition to me.

The Youth Officer asked Winston why he wanted Mr O'C. to go. Winston said,

"All us lot want him to go. He's no good for a Youth Leader. He can't manage us lot, an' when he got cold feet he called the weight-trainers, what was our mates, to beat us up; that's no good, setting mates against mates. An' last thing, what right's he got to talk to a kid the way he talked to our Titch? He didn't have no proof that Titch was meanin' to take that pop without payin' for it."

These were valid points enough. The Youth Officer and I promised that the matter of the petition should be looked into.

In point of fact the Youth Officer had already arranged for Driscoll to be transferred to another, less unclubable, club.

Winston now put in several nights of sterling work as leader of the party repairing damage at the Club. He then took an evening off, got drunk and assaulted a copper. For this he was fined five pounds. He asked for six months in which to pay and was given six weeks. This story appeared on the front-page of our local newspaper and at once established Winston as a hero.

Newspaper-editors would argue, I suppose, that publicity of

this sort exposes delinquents to public opprobrium and is therefore shame-making for them. In fact the reverse is true; newspaper publicity gives the wrongdoers celebrity-rating in the eyes of their cronies. Winston, far from slinking into the Club after this bannerline publicity, came swaggering in, proud as punch, just as Rory had swaggered in after he had knocked down his first copper.

I reflected that, for these boys, knocking down a copper was a species of initiation rite into the status of manhood. It was the equivalent of the Masai custom whereby every youth, on attaining a certain age, had to prove himself by spearing a lion single-handed. We had no lions, so our budding warriors knocked down coppers.

These boys at our Club were certainly physically tough. Skid, who had had his face so badly injured by the kicked-in lavatory door, was only a couple of days later playing in an inter-club handball match.

The basic atmosphere of the Club remained trouble-ripe. Several evenings Figgy, now back from her holiday, had to close early because of bad behaviour. Yet in spite of all this she was optimistic. She declared that she was getting the feel of the members and that the Club, she was certain, was about to take a turn for the better. She said that the members were at last starting to respond to her.

A big new road was being built through our town and many of the old, small houses in which our members lived were being demolished, their occupants moving out to new estates several miles distant from us. The Patcheys went, and the Chooseys, amongst others.

"Where have all the Patcheys gone?" asked the Treasurer. "Moved to a new estate out in the country," said Figgy. "And the Chooseys too, as well as one or two others of their set."

"Ye gods! What bliss! Shot of that mob!" said the Treasurer. "I thought things were remarkably peaceful down here. Now I know why."

"There's a new, forty-thousand pound youth-club near them, complete with barbecue and beauty-parlour," said Figgy. "So Patcheys and Chooseys will no doubt flock to that. Poor Ernest will find himself landed with them."

Poor Ernest was the Leader of the forty-thousand pound club. Imagine then the astonishment of us all when one evening there trooped into the Club the entire Patchey and Choosey offspring with the exception of Winston and Camilla.

I was on duty in the canteen. Estella Patchey (who had been allowed to join the Club somewhat under age in the first place because if she had not joined she would have been the only member of the Patchey children who didn't come to us and would have felt fearfully left out) came up to the canteen-counter and asked in her husky voice for a glass of water (no charge). She sipped the water for a moment or two, then embarked on one of those fascinating monologues that were her notion of conversation.

"It cost us ever such a lot to get here, we live so far away now. Ten-and-threepence for the lot, no, that's a lie, eleven-and-threepence; including there *and* back that'll be over a quid for the lot of us, ev'ry time we come. So we shan't be able to come ev'ry night like we used. Still, we wanted to come back ever so badly. We don't half miss living here. Camilla's gone to look at our old house. We lived in that house twenty-five years. We was all born there 'cept Winston. He was born on a island, 'cos of the war."

She didn't elucidate which island. Ireland perhaps? She took two or three more sips of water, then continued, "Mind you, our new house is smashing; but it's ever so quiet. I mean, it's really the country like. I mean, there's nothing to do if you're young, you know? They 'ave got a youth-club there, but it's nowhere near as good as this one. There's nothing to do at it. The little 'uns there, they jus' play games an' that, you know? An' the older ones, they sit an' talk about their income-tax. So we'd all rather come back here. There's more life to it.

"Winston's gone out with his mates. He's sold his old motor-bike. Got ninety quid for it! He give my Mum a smashing present an' all. You'll never guess what."

She looked happily at me, waiting for me to guess. I thought. Ninety quid. A washing-machine? No. Vacuum-cleaner? No. Electric-iron? No. With each no Estella shook her head vigorously. I said, "Then I give up."

"Whacking great bar of choclit! Biggest I ever see." She held out her hands, indicating a bar a couple of feet in length. "Straight." Nodding her head hard. "Gi-gan-tick."

Pause, while the drama of this gift sank in. Then,

"The garden of our new house is ever so big. It's got fuckin' great weeds in it, up to your chin, and them long things with corns stickin' out of 'em what scratch.* We'll all have to do gardening, my Mum says.

"An' you know what? We got a little kitten. It's called Kitty. Coo, 'sever so sweet! An' it's got a blue dish with *Kitty* wrote on it for its milk. You should see it; dish is bigger than the kitten. But it'll grow. My Mum says it's a girl kitten so it'll have lots of kittens of its own. Then we'll all have a kitty each! Mum'll have a kitty. Dad'll have a kitty. Camilla'll have a kitty. Winston'll have a kitty. Humph'll have a kitty. Paulette'll have a kitty. Titch'll have a kitty an' *I'll* have a kitty! See all them kitties! Bitta luck, all them kitties will have kitties of their own. Then we'll give Auntie one. An' Uncle one. An' Esme. An' Gaylord an' Kev an' Jeanette an' Jo-Anne an' Franchie an' Shirley an' Mick an' Clark an' Melanie an' Hayley an' an' an' whatsa baby? Oh yes, Evangeline. Funny name innit? You evverreard it afore?"

"Yes, it's a pretty name. How old's Evangeline?"

"Two. 'Ere, I got some smashin' new mates at my new school what I go to now. My two best mates are Sandra an' Cindy. They walk to school with me. But we don't half have to walk a long way to get there! My Mum says the council oughter provide a bus. An' the mud! You should see it! 'cos they an't made all the estate up yet, see? There's fields backa our house, with pigs. Cor, they pong. An' there's cows. An' horses at a ridin'-school. One of these horses got out its field and come in our garden one night last week and we heard it in the night, chewin'. It'd gone in the mornin' though, when we got up. Winston said if he'd found it in the garden he'da rode it.

"There's tall trees too, with nests in. An', an' there's wild flowers. An' we got green bathroom curtains with sea-'orses on 'em. An' yellow-bath-mat with a black footmark on it! We got that as a house-warming present."

A number of senior members now came into the canteen and began discussing a projected trip to Bognor. This bored Estella, she went to twist.

The older kids all loved Bognor. They planned to spend a day at the Butlin's camp there. Bertie was the only one who disliked this idea. He said,

"There's nothin' at them Butlins. Them places is dead. And

* She meant brambles.

everythin' costs three times as much as it do outside. You pay at least three-an'-six for your dinner. An' a fortune for ice-cream. I mean, you're puttin' it all in old Billy Butlin's pocket, right?"

But the others were all mad keen on Butlins. They said once you were inside it was a dead bargain and you could have a smashing time there all day without ever having to come outside again. And if it rained you didn't have to get wet. So Butlin's it was.

Our Club was now becoming the In-Club with the local Rocks; more members joined and we had a nightly average attendance of sixty, which was encouraging.

A heat-wave arrived, sultry and dusty. The kids became, as they always did in hot weather, both lethargic and tense. Their bodies slackened in the heat; their nerves tautened.

Rowenna was proving very popular with the boys. Mark was deeply smitten by her, but she was a wicked little flirt and almost drove the poor boy mad by first drawing him on and then switching her attentions to someone else. She made up to Bertie, Stoker, Grant. Mark fought them all. Bertie made himself scarce for a bit, but Stoker and Grant each had a real rough-house with Mark.

Then two new Rock girls joined; Liz and Queenie. Liz was plump, Queenie thin. Liz giggled and was silent, Queenie squealed and was vociferous. Stoker took an immediate fancy to Liz. This made Rowenna jealous; she liked to have all the boys to herself.

These quarrels and jealousies kept Figgy and her part-time Leaders busy. Clem had now come to us as a part-time assistant Leader; it was nice to have him around again. He dressed very smartly and was extremely adult, but underneath he hadn't changed very much.

In mid-July, when the sky looked and smelled of thunder, a boy from Romford came into the Club and made advances to Rowenna. He had met her, apparently, on the trip to Bognor. Romford was a long way from us, but the youth was so enchanted by Rowenna that distance was no object with him. Rowenna and Mark had just become unofficially engaged, so that when the Romford youth was found ogling Rowenna in our canteen Mark took strong and immediate objection. There was a fight, and the Romford boy beat a retreat.

Next night he returned with a party of supporters. They

meant real business. They arrived in cars, which they parked so that they blocked the street exit from our Club. Then, armed with crowbars, they entered the Club, grabbed Mark who was seated in the canteen, dragged him outside and beat him up.

Figgy ran out to Mark's assistance; a youth shoved a crowbar in her stomach and pushed her back. She said afterwards that she was sure that a male Leader would have been beaten up. Her one thought was to save Mark, but she realized that for her to be injured would achieve nothing, so she ran very quickly back into the Club, before her assailant grasped what she was up to, and rang the police.

The police had learned, by heaven knows what grapevine, that there was going to be a bust-up at our Club, so they were anticipating a call and were therefore on the scene of action with great promptitude.

Meantime Winston Patchey and Al Choosey had gathered a handful of personal troops with which they attacked a contingent of the enemy, who were routed and ran to escape in a car. Winston went careering after them, armed with a navvy's shovel; he was seized, bundled into the car and beaten up in the back seat as the car drove off. The onlookers had a glimpse of arms, legs and shovel all going madly at once; the back window was smashed and the shovel flew out into the street. Aloysius and three relatives leapt on their bikes and gave chase to the car.

At this point the police arrived. The rest of the Romford boys at once tried to escape, throwing their weapons into front gardens as they ran; the neighbours fetched to the Club next day a collection of crow-bars, choppers and bicycle-chains which they had found amongst their privets and laurels. Fifteen of the Romford boys were caught and appeared before the magistrates.

Mark, who had been left bleeding on the pavement, was taken to hospital where he was treated for a broken nose and a lacerated scalp.

Winston and Al had finished up the evening in a quiet backwater of far-flung suburbia where they and Winston's captors had enjoyed a good scrap without police intervention; at least, this is what Winston told us had happened, but it was difficult to extract the details. Someone else reported that the police had intervened and that both Winston and Al had assaulted a copper.

An account of the evening's shindigs appeared in a national evening newspaper which described our Club as "a club for moderate Rocks."

The evening after the fight a policeman with a dog patrolled outside the Club in case of more trouble, but things remained quiet. The Patcheys and the Chooseys stayed away, with the exception of Camilla and Estella Patchey, and Esme Choosey, who were, we suspected, sent along as spies by their battling brothers.

Several of the non-fighting members of the Club called in early to say that they wouldn't be down at the Club tonight, they were going to the cinema. We guessed that their parents had put the Club out of bounds.

Figgy was upset by the fight; its occurrence had dismayed her because she had been thinking that she had at last got the feel of the members and that the Club had taken a big turn for the better.

At the same time she confessed that she also felt oddly cheered by the fact that she had had a really bad experience at the Club, the kind of experience that all youth leaders dread; she had come out of it much better than she had expected. "You know, you always wonder how you'll react to a thing like that; how scared you'll be and so on. At the time it was happening I wasn't so scared as I thought I might be; it was afterwards that I felt awful, got the shivers and the shakes. I was more angry with those Romford boys than frightened of them; it made me so mad to see a gang of them like that all set on poor Mark, and us not able to do anything to help him."

We decided that if we had any more serious trouble we would close the Club for a week or so, to let things simmer down.

We were rather afraid that the Romford boys might return for reprisals against Winston and Al. For this reason Figgy was not particularly keen to have these two boys in the Club and since they were both in arrears with their subs she decided to make this an excuse for keeping them out of the Club for a while. The idea fell flat, however. Winston and Al turned up with a friend whom they wished to introduce as a new member. He was a tough, longish-haired youth in excessively tight jeans; Figgy was not anxious to have him as a member. So she said that neither Winston nor Al could come into the Club, let alone introduce a friend, because they were several weeks in arrears.

The friend, to whom money seemed to be no object, thereupon paid all the back subscription money and his own entry-fee, thereby quite cutting the ground from under poor Figgy's feet.

The newcomer did not make at all a happy first impression. The first thing that he did was to attempt to break down the locked door of the Leader's office. "Jus' wanted to see what was inside."

How misleading first impressions can be! This boy subsequently became one of our most loyal and helpful members.

Figgy confessed to me that she was scared of Winston and Aloysius. I confessed that I was scared of them also. They were, each of them, only slight in build, but very wiry and strong. Their locks were wild, their jeans worn, their black plastic jackets were intricately patterned with brass studs. They were both intelligent, gay, and entirely intimidating.

Still, if one allows oneself to be intimidated all is lost. Figgy persevered with them and in due course announced to me that she was beginning to know how to handle them. I was mainly confined to dealing with them in the canteen, which wasn't such a problem, but I can't say that I ever felt entirely at ease with Aloysius, although I did become quite friendly with Winston, who was a nice boy, when he wasn't knocking people flat with his fists. His knuckles were permanently red and swollen from fighting.

The story in the evening paper, which gave our Club such dubious publicity, much pleased the members, especially Bertie, who once again was heard suggesting, "Let's us Rocks go down to the coffee-bar and beat up some of them Mods, shall we?" But I was tempted to think that he preferred talking about fighting to the actual thing, for on the night of the big fight at the Club he had not played an active part and he had been careful not to come down to the Club for two or three nights after it.

When he had first joined the Club he had been quite one of our most taciturn members, but now he had jollied up a lot and was downright chatty and much given to loud, chuckling laughter. He was put on the Members' Committee and handed various responsibilities.

We were trying to conduct an anti-cigarette campaign. The Youth Officer provided us with some frightening posters and a lecturer, who illustrated his talk with a real carcinomatous lung pickled in a jar. But so far as most of the members were concerned this sort of propaganda went in at one ear and came out at the other; they all smoked like chimneys (we now, 1966, notice that they don't smoke so much).

Bertie was a chain-smoker and poo'poo'd all talk of connection between cigarettes and lung-cancer. He was fond of spreading himself full-length on a bench, a cigarette in one hand and a bottle of coke in the other, and holding forth to the company in general that smoking fags don't cause cancer, mate, it's the gases what was released into the atmosphere from the bombs in the last war what do it.

I said, "Where on earth did you get that from?"

"Read it in a Sunday newspaper."

"Can you read?" asked Winston politely.

" 'Cors I can read, you berk," roared Bertie.

"He knows the diff'rence atween 'Gents' an' 'Ladies', don't you Bertie?"

"Yeah, mate, but he didn't find it out through readin'!"

And so on.

"That there whatsit, what was in that jar, warn't genooin," said Bertie.

"That lung, d'you mean?"

"Yeah. Warn't real."

"What makes you think that?" I asked.

"They don't look like that mate; that was plaster."

"How d'you know?"

"Well, stands to reason, it'd go bad if it was real."

"It was put in somethin' special to keep it, you steamin' twit," said Queenie.

"The trouble with you, Bertie, is that you don't want to believe that cigarettes may give you lung cancer, so you refuse to believe it," said Figgy.

"Orright mate, when I'm dyin' of lung cancer I'll come along to you an' Mrs B. an' I'll say, 'Orright, you won, I'm dyin' of lung cancer'. Fair enough?"

"Horrid thing to die of, Bertie."

"Ergh, you'll die in the end whatever you do, mate, so may as well die of somethin' you enjoy doin'. Right?"

A rumour came through that the Romford boys were planning another raid. They were after Winston and Al.

I went down to the Club on the night of the rumoured attack;

I felt that if Figgy had the guts to be there I should be there too. The place was very quiet. The evening was hot. The juke-box wasn't playing, for a change; one could hear the table-tennis ball skipping back and forth erratically on the table and a hum of conversation punctuated by squeals from Queenie.

Figgy greeted me. She said, "If trouble does come it won't be until half-past nine or so. That's when it comes. But the police have been patrolling and I don't think anything will happen. Anyway, Gus and I have got a really good hold on the members now; I don't mean we're oppressing them or anything, but I mean we both feel we can handle them now. I suppose it's all just a matter of getting one's confidence. Like any other job in life."

She paused, then went on, "Still, I don't think we'll be taken by surprise like we were last time they came. Last time they dashed in here and lugged out poor Mark before I'd even realized what was going on. But now Gus and I patrol around the front-door a good deal, and all the members know that if anything does happen they mustn't scream and mill around like they did last time, but come and tell me immediately, and I'll telephone the police right away."

At twenty-five-to-ten we noticed Grant come in, looking rather tense. He went to Winston, who was drinking cokes in the canteen. Winston immediately slipped out of the Club and drove off on his bike.

"Making himself scarce," murmured Figgy. "I wonder if that means they're on their way here?"

Grant, Mark and Al now left the Club. Then Bertie lumbered out.

"Let's go and stand outside," said Figgy. "They'll think twice about barging in here and causing trouble if they see me."

With which sublime remark the little woman marched out on to the pavement. I lit a cigarette and followed her. I felt distinctly nervous.

Figgy stood on the pavement surveying the street, which was gradually fading into smokey dusk. Sounds of voices came from open windows, music, babies wailing. In the distance the traffic swept along. Figgy said, "A police patrol-car has just gone past; I don't think we shall get any trouble tonight. Still, best wait and see for a while longer. They won't find anyone here that they want, even if they do come."

As we stood waiting we chatted. Figgy said, "My husband thinks I've gone daft doing this job. After the attack the other night he said, 'Well, now you'll pack it in, won't you?' But I said no, now that I've been through the worst and come out the other side I know I'm going to keep on with the job, because I wasn't certain before that I really could handle the type of member we get down here, but now I'm beginning to feel that I really can. For several nights afterwards I just turned all cold every time I thought of that fight, and poor Mark, but now I feel quite normal about it, so I reckon I am going to be all right."

"I was looking at Mark this evening," I said. "Apart from being a bit pale he seems O.K. again."

"They're incredibly tough, these kids. Because he was quite badly hurt. He says his nose is still rather sore."

"Had Rowenna led the other boy on, d'you think?"

"I expect so. She's a real little baggage. Yet she can be a sweet kid when she chooses. Like so many of 'em." I started another cigarette. It was quickly growing darker. The street lamps were on. One couldn't see how dark the sky really was because of the red glare which illuminated the coming night from horizon to horizon; the glare of the vast, built-up plain which lay around us, quivering with lights and aching with sound. There is no rest at night in the so-called civilized world.

"The worst thing, the other evening, was seeing them beating up poor Mark; all of them beating him, you know, and us quite helpless to stop them. That was what made me feel sick," she said. "You know, it was like being with savages."

The church clock struck a quarter-to-ten.

"How did the members react to you fetching the coppers?" I asked.

"That's the funny thing, none of them seemed to mind. I thought some of them might remark on it afterwards, you know, 'She called the rozzers.' But they didn't. Well I've told them that it's my job to protect the Club, the Club comes first with me. Matter of fact one of the Choosey boys did ask me whose side I was on. Meaning was I on the side of the kids or the side of the law. I said I'm on the side of the Club; and that means in effect that I'm on the side of *all* the members, not just siding with one or two individuals in their private battles with the law. I have no part in private battles. I'm on the side of the Club.

That means I'm on the side of the law, because the Club mustn't break the law. So if that finds me one side of the fence and some individual member on the other side of the fence it's just too bad. I'm still that boy's friend, and I'll do what I can to help him, but I won't side with that boy against the law. They seem to think that's fair enough."

A motor-bike came coasting slowly down the street, its engine softly throbbing, its driver apparently merely staring at us casually, in reality very intently. He glided by; the bike's aerial quivered, a cat's alert whisker; then the bike had passed, its rear-light glowing and dwindling like a delivered message. Behind came another with a pillion-rider behind the driver. They too drifted past, followed by a third bike. Then came a brief pause, then four more bikes. The riders surveyed us in the intently keen, yet indirectly staring manner of animals. The bikes throbbed away up the street, aerials quivering, rear-lights red-eyed.

"Recognize any of them?" I asked Figgy.

"No. All strangers. I bet they're looking for Winston."

We remained outside the Club, still talking. The bikes returned, throbbed past as before. It was night now. Dark shadow engulfed each end of the street and the lights at the windows and the voices and music were switched abruptly off, one after the other, as people went to bed. It was a street where people retired early.

Once again the bikes went by; the faces of the riders, turned towards us, were now merely blurs in the poor light. The sultry air grew cooler with a small breeze. Some tobacco-plants in a garden smelt sweet and strong. We waited a bit longer, each of us folding our bare arms and hugging ourselves and moving our feet because it was no longer warm out there on the pavement. The bikes didn't return, so we went inside the Club again. Here we found Gus closing the canteen. The few members who were left said good-night and departed. We three adults chatted a little, then closed the Club and went home.

The police continued, most helpfully, to patrol the streets round the Club at regular intervals each evening, in case of trouble, but the enemy from Romford didn't show up again.

And now the time had come to hold our week-end camp at a bosky site in wildest Sussex. It was to be a mixed camp this year; the first time we had ever tried one. Our previous Leaders, male, had not felt up to handling girls in a camp as well as boys; for Figgy, of course, the girls presented no problem and she was blithely certain that she could manage the boys.

The weather was hot and the camp was clearly going to be fun, with walking on the Downs and bathing in the sea. Camilla Patchey and Rowenna swore that they would pack topless swim-suits. Figgy said that topless swim-suits would be banned. Everyone began to shout, "Oh be a sport!" and "Why spoil our fun?" and Camilla said she didn't care if they were banned, she'd still be wearing one.

But it all turned out to be talk. Nobody packed topless swim-suits.

Figgy saw to it that the tents of the camp were pitched in two distinct groups and on the first night she made certain that when everyone settled down the boys were strictly in their part of the camp and the girls in theirs. But ten minutes after *Lights Out* she heard girls' voices coming from one of the boys' tents, so she popped over to see what was happening. Figgy found two of the girls cheerfully sacked down with two of the boys. "Come on, cut that out," said Figgy. One of the boys, from within his sack, begged urgently for "just ten minutes more."

"Not on your sweet life," said Figgy. "Too much can happen in ten minutes, mate." And so saying she seized the girl and yanked her from the sack.

The second night the girls unanimously requested Figgy to sleep in their tent with them. Apparently a mass male raid on the females had been planned and it was not welcome.

There were no other troubles of any kind, and as Figgy said you really couldn't call these troubles. One expected a certain amount of larking about. And she, together with Gus and Clem, had had everything under control.

And this was the incredible thing: Figgy had got everything under control, at all events as much as one ever can, or should, get effervescent youth under control. She had not got them clamped down under an autocratic regime; we had learned that that didn't work. We had learned, too, that the permissive approach didn't work and Figgy was careful to avoid that. She had achieved a democratic balance.

She appealed to the spirit of reasonable compromise which is such an impressive feature of British teen-agers, especially these tougher groups. When a problem blew up Figgy said,

"Now see here, you lot, I simply can't allow such-and-such; surely you yourselves can see that? So I suggest this, that, or the other compromise way out." And the kids would listen and think a bit and then say, "Right-oh, Figgy, we get your point. Yeah, fair enough Figgy. We'll go with that." And so they would go with it.

They had a keen sense of justice. If they thought that you were giving them a square deal then they would give you a square deal. But if they thought that you weren't on the level with them, or were being patronizing, or were wet, then you had had it.

Figgy understood all this. She was entirely in sympathy with them. She knew, instinctively, how to combine firm handling with sincere affection.

She knew how to give them the kind of Club that they wanted, and needed, without either succumbing to them over points of primary discipline, or forcing anything upon them. She could be flexible, yet control them.

Their fondness for her was revealed not only in the manner in which they spoke to her and treated her, but also by the tone in which they spoke of her when she was not there. On one occasion when she was absent on a training-course Stoker asked me, impatiently and wistfully, "Where's our l'il ole Fig?"

On the other hand even the toughest boys held her in an impressive, yet oddly touching, awe. Winston said to Skid, "You look out, mate; mind ole Figgy doan' catch you doin' that or you'll cop it." And Winston meant it as a serious warning.

The girls were equally well attuned to her. They enjoyed doing things with her, and for her, but they particularly loved it if she did little personal things for them. She was a versatile woman, having trained as a chiropodist as well as a youth-leader, and she was also a skilled needlewoman and handy at hair-dressing. So one would hear the girls calling, "Figgy, when you gonna do my corns?" "Fig, when you gonna set my hair?" "Figgy, when you gonna show me featherstitching?" Or, learn me badminton, take us swimming?

But then perhaps you would hear Rowenna say to Queenie, " 'ere, look out, 'ere comes Mrs Figg, she'll have your life for that, mate." And Queenie would look out without delay.

They all basked in l'il ole Fig's smiles, and feared l'il ole Fig's wrath. And when the time came for us to choose our full-time

Leader for the future Centre, we asked for, and got, l'il ole Fig.

In those last weeks of July we had also reached our last weeks as a full working Club at the old premises. In September we should move; Figgy and I spent much time planning and organizing. She was full of practical schemes and knew how to put them through. She was determined that the members should help with the moving. At the moment she had them cleaning and repainting some of the furniture we would take with us.

Fighting was still continuing sporadically; Winston and Aloysius attracted fighters, some as henchmen, some as adversaries. Although the Romford boys never returned to the Club to attack, we knew that Winston and Al were constantly involved in fights, all over the place.

Not all of these were with other boys, either. At the end of the month Aloysius was remanded in custody for a fortnight for assaulting a policeman; it transpired that this was the sixth copper he had knocked about in so many weeks.

"A copper a week
    Ends you up with the Beak,"

sang Titch Patchey.

Aloysius had been mixing it with cops in localities as far apart as Southend and Wood Green. He also owed a considerable sum in accumulated police-court fines.

Winston was still running free, but as Skid said, "That bloke'll find himself in the cooler too before very much longer."

Figgy had been in two minds about holding the big dance with which we had planned to wind-up our tenancy of the old Club premises. Aloysius and Winston had been attracting such wild types to the Club recently that a dance had seemed pretty inadvisable. But with Aloysius in custody and Winston treading rather delicately in case he followed, Figgy decided to go ahead with the dance. We wanted to finish up with a good night, a night everyone would remember pleasantly.

We had engaged a live group, but they let us down at the last moment, so we resorted to the juke-box and the Rolling Stones top-of-the-hit-parade disc sent all the kids into a stomping frenzy which beat all noise we had hitherto heard down there. In the middle of it Mrs X. turned up. She looked even more white and indignant and distraught than she normally looked on such occasions. Figgy, blaming it on the Stones, advanced to Mrs X. and began explaining sweetly that it was our closing dance and all noise would cease, for ever more, on the dot of ten-thirty. But Mrs X. was complaining of something other than noise. Her husband had just been found lying toes up in the passageway between her house and the Club; he was out stone-cold and the culprit, declared Mrs X., was one of our members. She didn't doubt for one minute, she said, that her old man, who had been on his way to us to complain about the noise, had met one of our young villains in the passage and had been knocked down.

To be honest, we didn't doubt it either, but as there was not a shred of evidence to support her allegation we refused to become involved in the matter. Figgy advised her to go to the police.

Mr X. remained unconscious for several hours. When he came round he had no memory of what had happened, so nobody ever did find out who knocked him down, although naturally everybody had their suspicions.

Thus, with the Stones rolling and the kids stomping and Mr X. flat out and Mrs X. distraught and calling the police and the neighbours seething over it all there ended our last dance of our final session at the old Club.

PART SIX

A GOOD CLUB TO JOIN

"The society that prefers the kind of man who has never examined the meaning of his life against the context in which he lives is bound to believe that it has a youth problem. For its own sake, and the sake of its social future, one can only pray that it really does have."

Edgar Z. Friedenberg. *Coming of Age in America.*
(Random House)

CHAPTER XVI

A GOOD CLUB TO JOIN

OUR MOVE TO the new premises was now scheduled, definitely, for the end of September.

The Management Committee (the survivors of our old committee reinforced by a senior probation officer, a police inspector, a J.P. from juvenile court, a woman welfare officer, a worker amongst deprived children, three or four local business men with an active interest in and first-hand experience of modern club work, and two parents) held a preliminary meeting on the new premises.

I had planned it as an elegant business meeting followed by sherry. We had the sherry all right, but otherwise things were unconventional. A freak storm and cloud-burst occurred just before the meeting was due to start. Since the place was not yet furnished the Vice-Chairman had arranged to bring some chairs. The flooding prevented his van getting through and Figgy and I had to improvise benches from ladders workmen had left behind propped on old paint and petrol cans. The electricity was not yet switched on, the stormy evening was exceptionally dark; Figgy scuttled about borrowing hurricane-lamps from the Guides. Everyone had dressed smartly for such an auspicious first meeting; the combination of best suits, chic dresses, good sherry, polished glasses, ladders, petrol-cans and hurricane-lamps was inimitably us.

The meeting itself went well and we got a lot of planning and business done.

Lists had been made of the furniture, fittings and equipment that would be required for the new Club: Figgy had the final voice in all this and it was she who did all the ordering and purchasing after the local Education authority had approved the lists and financial grants had been made. The total estimated cost of equipment etcetera was £660; towards this we received a 75% grant. The remaining amount was our responsibility. We had, in fact, a pretty healthy bank balance by now, thanks to the efficiency of our Treasurer and various money-raising efforts made by the Management Committee. We were determined that our new Club should not be hamstrung in its development, as the old one had been, by meagre finances. Although our new Club would not, by any standards, be rich, at least it would not stagger into the arena on its uppers.

Of course we had the usual offers of old armchairs, carpets and upright pianos from so-called well-wishers. I enjoyed dealing with these; scintillating telephone-conversations took place between myself and the intending donors who, by god, must have said hard things about me afterwards. Nobody likes being told that their old junk isn't wanted. You can tell a person, without giving any offence, that you don't want the loan of their Rolls-Royce, but try telling them that you don't want the gift of their forty-year-old dining-room suite!

Figgy and I were adamant; we were not having any old armchairs, carpets, pianos. Absolutely no tat, we swore, was to enter the new premises. We were only bringing away from the old Club equipment that was in good shape, and decent furniture.

When we reopened after the August recess Figgy reserved some evenings for selected working-parties of senior members who helped her sort equipment, compose an inventory, clean and redecorate furniture that was being taken with us, and spruce up the old premises so that they might be left in decent order.

All the familiar faces turned up to assist, with the exception of Winston and Aloysius. They had both gone to Borstal.

Several of our former Mod members rejoined; they were keen to belong to the new Club.

The kids were all being very happy, relaxed, co-operative and, for them, pretty good and quiet. Figgy explained that she was at last beginning to get the real feel of them.

We had scarcely been open for a week after the recess when tragedy struck; Stoker was killed on his new motor-bike. Since he had been a very active and popular member his death was a real blow. He had been a great one for organizing collections; for Club discs, for Oxfam, for spastics, for thalidomide babies; rattle rattle clink clink, come on duck, give us a tosheroon, it's a bleedin' fabulous cause. Now we collected for Stoker. The money rolled in and the wreath we bought was big and beautiful.

Everybody turned up at the cemetery where Stoker, by

painful irony, had himself worked not so long ago as a grave-digger, developing his muscles for whaling.

My most vivid memory of the boy was the occasion when he had offered himself as a prize in a Club raffle. We had been a prize short and Stoker had come up with the brilliant suggestion: "Tell you what, Mrs B., 'ave me as a first prize."

"Wonderful, but what precisely does the lucky winner do with you? Stuff you? Keep you on the sideboard as a souvenir?"

"Yeah; keep me with the family heirlooms. No but seriously, Mrs B., old Carrots an' me will be a smashin' first prize; we'll go to the person's house, what wins us, in our spare time for a fortnight and springclean the place for them, top to bottom. How's that?"

It was a great idea, although it didn't come off because somebody produced a bottle of whisky as first prize instead. A pity, really. To have won Stoker and Carrots would have been fun.

And now Stoker was dead.

Although nobody talked about him much, openly, afterwards he was in fact remembered for a long time. Carrots ceased to come to the Club.

On September 25th we moved. Figgy and I had discussed, half jokingly, half seriously, how we should go in a triumphant procession through the town, from the old premises to the new, with banners, a motor-bike escort, and a band playing "When the Saints Come Marching In." But of course it didn't turn out like that. We moved hurriedly, almost furtively. The landlord wanted us out quickly; he had relet the premises. The new Club was not completely ready; almost, not quite. We had not wanted to move until everything awaited us just-so, but we had no choice.

We managed to hire a lorry and with the help of the kids we transported the furniture and equipment round to the new Club. The members looked utterly thrilled, almost to the point of being stunned, when they saw the new place. It was really touching to see the smiles on their faces as they stood in the new canteen and stared about them.

Some of our senior boys had been to school there. So had our lorry-driver. He said, "I used to be here when I was a little nipper. But it warn't like this then. Blimey, they do things nice for kids nowadays, don't they?"

Ian, who had also been to school there, said, "It's nice to be back, an' find it done up so posh. Nice it to be a place you know, only made more modern."

The kids, Gus, Figgy, the Youth Officer, the lorry-driver and I brought all the things from the lorry, which had to make two trips, into the new Club and dumped them in the foyer and the Leader's Office. At last the move was completed and most of the people went away. I stood in the foyer, looking at the pile of stuff. Then I groaned to Figgy, "My god, they've fetched all the old junk that we said was to be left behind."

Unspeakable old chests-of-drawers, groggy cupboards, rickety tables, old boxes, broken benches and lidless bins; the lot. All the rotten old objects that Figgy and I had planned to jettison. Here they were.

"It's hopeless," I said. "You can never cut out the past of your life. Even physical junk has a mysterious adhesive quality, let alone all the other, emotional, things."

I sat down on a chair beside a battered old tool-chest that Brian had brought with him to the Club five years ago; I picked up Skip's old climbing-rope that lay in a jumble on the floor and began coiling it. "There's never any such thing, really, as a fresh start, a clean break."

"We'll just have to have a bonfire in the yard," said Figgy.

Together we humped and lumped the stuff into the yard. We got fearfully grimy. Since the water-supply was not yet turned on we couldn't wash our hands; we couldn't even make a cup of tea.

The afternoon now had almost a feeling of anti-climax. One had thought so much about this moment when we would step into the new Club. Now here we were covering ourselves with dust from shabby old objects from which I, at all events, had been picking up dust since the Club first started. But Figgy kept saying, "We shall be able to do this down here; we shall be able to do that down here" and of course she was right; it was a marvellous, optimistic moment in spite of all the old junk we were grimly shoving around.

For the first few evenings everything was pretty quiet; our old members came in and helped arrange furniture, organize the office, the canteen, house equipment. The boys burned and chopped the junk that Figgy and I found so irksome. The girls ran up curtains for the windows. We didn't attempt, as yet, to enrol any new members.

Then we did open our doors to new applicants and they arrived in a steady stream. We had furnished a fresh supply of application-forms; the kids queued at the office window, filling them in very seriously and thoughtfully. I read the forms as they were handed in.

One said that his occupation was plumber's apprentice, his hobby birds, his religion agnostic and he wanted to join the Club because his mates had joined it.

The next said he worked on a building-site, his hobby was folk-music, he was an atheist and he wanted to join the Club because he thought it was a good club to join.

The next said he was a trainee engineer, no hobbies except doing nothing, religion agnostic, and he wanted to join the Club because his mates belonged and said it was a good club to join.

The next said that he was a student, his hobby foreign travel, he was an atheist, and wanted to join the Club because he had been told it was a good club.

The next was a Congregationalist, his hobby was jazz, he was taking A-levels and wanted to join because his girl friend was a member.

And so on.

Hardly anybody said that they were C. of E., like they so often used to put, and nobody seemed to join any more to get them off the streets.

These young people, when they applied to join us, felt that our application forms should be treated seriously and that they should, in reply to our questions, say what they really felt and really wanted to say, instead of what they believed we wanted them to say.

Since many of them were at the age when large numbers of young people pass through a period of atheism or agnosticism they said that they were atheists or agnostics.

As for so many of them saying they wanted to join because they had been told that it was a good club to join, well, that was pretty marvellous because it meant that after five years of hard work, hard trying and hard learning we were actually getting somewhere.